The Ministry of the Spirit

The Ministry of the Spirit

A.J. GORDON

BETHANY HOUSE PUBLISHERS
MINNEAPOLIS, MINNESOTA 55438
A Division of Bethany Fellowship, Inc.

Published by Bethany House Publishers
A Division of Bethany Fellowship, Inc.
6820 Auto Club Road, Minneapolis, Minnesota 55438

Printed in the United States of America

Library of Congress Cataloging in Publication Data

Gordon, A. J. (Adoniram Judson), 1836-1895.
    The ministry of the Spirit.

    1. Holy Spirit.   I. Title.
BT121.2.G67   1985,   231'.3   85-27503
ISBN 0-87123-843-8

ADONIRAM JUDSON GORDON (1836–1895) was a Baptist minister, educator, and author. He graduated from Brown University (1860) and Newton Theological Seminary (1863), and for six years was minister of Jamaica Plain (Massachusetts) Baptist Church. In 1869 he went to Clarendon Street Baptist Church, Boston, a center of evangelistic work. He founded a school for training missionaries for home and foreign service, and for pastors' assistants, from which came Gordon College and its divinity school. His writings include *The Ministry of Healing, The Ministry of the Spirit*, and *When Christ Came to Church*.

Preface

In writing this small volume about the doctrine of the Holy Spirit, it cannot be claimed that all has been said that might be said on the subject. On the contrary, I proceeded to write with the belief that it was best to limit the sphere of discussion rather than extend it to the farthest bounds. So, though the subject of this book is in itself profoundly mysterious, we have sought to simplify it by concentrating on the present ministry of the Holy Spirit. What the Spirit did before the incarnation of Christ and what He may do after the second advent of Christ are questions hardly touched on in this volume. We have sought rather to emphasize and magnify the great truth that *the Paraclete—the Holy Spirit—is now present in the church*, that He has been poured out with all the unspeakable blessing for the church and for the world that this economy provides. As we speak of the ministry of Christ as a service with defined limits, so we now speak of the ministry of the Spirit as the work of the Comforter extending from Pentecost to the end of this dispensation.

How deep a subject for a study! What prayer is more appropriate than the humble petition that the Spirit himself will teach us concerning himself. Deeply aware of the limitations of this work, it is now committed to the use and blessing of that *divine person* of the Godhead of whom it so unworthily speaks.

A. J. Gordon
Boston, Massachusetts
December, 1894

Contents

Introduction

It is remarkable how much has been written recently about the Holy Spirit. Without a doubt the mind of the church is being instructed and her heart prepared for a recognition of the indwelling, administration, and cooperation of the blessed Paraclete. This instruction has never been surpassed in her history and holds the greatest promise both to her and to the world.

Each of these recent works has brought out some new phase of the person or mission of the Holy Spirit, but I cannot recall one that is so understandable, so scriptural, so deeply spiritual as this, by my beloved friend, Dr. Gordon. I found the chapters on the Embodying, the Enduement, and the Administration of the Spirit especially fresh and helpful. If these truths be stamped into the mental and spiritual constitution of God's servants, there would be such a revival of pure and undefiled religion and such marvelous results in the world that the age would close with a worldwide Pentecost. And this is clearly demonstrated to be in the purpose of God—nothing else can meet the deepest needs and yearnings of our time.

Christianity is beset with three powerful currents that subtly deflect her from her course: materialism, which denies or ignores the supernatural and concentrates on improving the outward conditions of human life; higher criticism, which is clever at analysis and dissection but unable to construct a foundation on which spiritual life may build and rest; and a fine literary taste, which is disposed to judge according to force of words or by delicacy of expression.

To all these we have but one reply: We offer them not a system, a creed, a church, but the living Christ, who was dead but is alive forevermore—He alone has the keys to unlock all perplexities, problems, and failures. Though society be restructured and material necessities more evenly supplied, discontent would break out again in some other form unless the hearts of people are satisfied with God's love. The truth that He reveals to the soul, and which is ensphered in Him, is alone able to answer the consuming questions of life and destiny and God, which are ever knocking at the mind's door for solution. Men have yet to learn that the highest power is not in words or bursts of eloquence but in the indwelling and outworking of Jesus Christ through the Holy Spirit.

Jesus Christ, the ever-living Son of God, is the one supreme answer to the restlessness of our day. But He cannot, He will not, reveal himself. Each person in the Trinity reveals another. The Son reveals the Father, but His own revelation awaits the testimony of the Holy Spirit. That testimony, though often given to individuals directly, is primarily given through the church. What we need then is the Son of God, revealed in all His radiant beauty through the ministry of the Holy Spirit.

Some seem to think that the Holy Spirit himself is the solution to the problems of our time. In this they err: during this age it is God in the person of Christ that is the one and only divine answer. Here is God's yes and amen, the Alpha and Omega, sight for the blind, cleansing for the polluted, life for the dead, the gospel for the poor and comfortless. Now we covet the gracious bestowal of the Spirit, that He may take more deeply of the things of Christ and reveal them to us. When the disciples sought to know the Father, the Lord said, "He that hath seen me hath seen the Father. It is His glory that shines on my face and His purpose that is fulfilled in my ministry." So the blessed Paraclete desires to turn our thought and attention from himself to Christ, one with Him in the Holy Trinity and the one He has come to reveal.

Throughout the centuries the voice of the Holy Spirit has borne witness to the Lord, directly and mediately. Directly, in each widespread quickening of the human conscience, each revival of religion, each era of advance in the knowledge of divine truth, and in each soul that has been regenerated, comforted, or taught. Mediately, His work has been carried on through the church, the body of those that believe. But, alas, how sadly His witness has been weakened and hindered by the medium through which it has come! He has not been able to do many mighty works because unbelief has kept closed those avenues through which He would have poured His glad testimony to the unseen and glorified Lord.

The divisions of the church, her strife about matters of comparative unimportance, her magnification of points of difference, her materialism, her love of money and place and power—all these have not only robbed the church of her testimony, but have grieved and quenched the Holy Spirit and nullified His testimony.

We gladly welcome the signs indicating that this period of apathy and resistance is coming to a close. The Church within the churches is making herself felt, arising from the dust and arraying herself in her beautiful garments. There is widespread recognition of the unity of all who believe, together with an increasing desire to magnify the points of agreement and minimize those of divergence. There are great conventions on both sides of the Atlantic for the quickening of spiritual life. Believers meet irrespective of name or group, doing an incalculable amount of good in breaking down the old lines of demarcation and making real our spiritual oneness. The teaching of consecration and cleanliness of heart and life is removing those obstacles that have restrained and drowned the

Spirit's still small voice. And as believers have become more consistent and devoted, they have grown increasingly sensitive to the indwelling, energy, and co-witness of the Holy Spirit.

If this movement is permitted to achieve its full purpose, the effect will be transcendently glorious. The church will become as easily usable to the Divine Tenant as the resurrection body of our Lord was to the impulse of His divine nature. And so Jesus will increasingly become the object of human hope, the Lord of all human life.

This book has been written that the Lord Jesus might be thus magnified and glorified through the ministry of the Holy Spirit and that the hearts and lives of believers might be made more sensitive to and receptive of His working. I add my testimony to the beloved author's, that in the mouth of two witnesses every word may be established. My prayer is that the witness of the Spirit to the great voice of the gospel may be heard more mightily and persistently among us.

F. B. Meyer

"It is evident that the present dispensation under which we are is the dispensation of the Spirit, or of the Third Person of the Holy Trinity. To him in the Divine economy has been committed the office of applying the redemption of the Son to the souls of men by the vocation, justification, and salvation of the elect. We are therefore under the personal guidance of the Third Person as truly as the apostles were under the guidance of the Second."

—Henry Edward Manning

1

The Age-Mission of the Spirit

A professor of theology has observed that little attention has been given to the person and work of the Holy Spirit compared to the wealth of material available on the life and ministry of Jesus Christ. It is affirmed, moreover, that in many of the present works on the subject there is a lack of clarity that leaves much to be desired in the treatment of this subject. These observations lead us to ask: Why not employ the same method in writing about the third Person of the Trinity as we use in considering the second Person? Scores of excellent works have been written on the life of Christ; we find that in these, almost without exception, the divine story begins with Bethlehem and ends with the Ascension. Though the Savior lived before His incarnation and continues to live after His ascension, it gives a certain definiteness of impression to limit one's view to His historic career, distinguishing His visible life lived in time from His invisible life lived in eternity.

So in considering the Holy Spirit, we believe there is an advantage in concentrating upon His ministry in time, bounding it by Pentecost on the one side and by Christ's second coming on the other. One of the best works on the Spirit I have found is by a Roman Catholic—Cardinal Manning. Notwithstanding his Catholic bias, his general conception of the subject is in some particulars admirable. His work is called *The Temporal Mission of the Holy Ghost*. How much is suggested by this title! Just as Jesus Christ had a time-ministry which He came into the world to fulfill, and having accomplished it returned to the Father, so the Holy Spirit for the fulfillment of a definite mission came into the world at an appointed time. He is now carrying on His ministry on earth, and in due time He will complete it and ascend to heaven again—this is what Manning's title suggests. This is what, we believe, the Scriptures teach. If we understand the present age-ministry of the Spirit, we have a definite viewpoint from which to study His operations in past ages and His greater mission, if there be such, in the ages to come.

The Holy Spirit's present time-ministry is clear in Scripture—a ministry with a definite beginning and a definite termination. In His farewell discourse, Christ made it clear that just as His own advent was foretold by prophets and angels, He now announced the advent into the world of another, coequal with himself, His divine successor, his other self in the unity of the Godhead. Moreover, it seems clear that He implied that this coming One was to appear not only for an appointed work but for an appointed period: "He shall give you another Comforter, that he may abide with you forever" (John 14:16). If we translate "forever" literally and say "*for the age*," it harmonizes with a parallel passage. In giving the great commission, Jesus says: "And lo, I am with you always, even *unto the end of the age*" (Matt. 28:20). His presence by the Holy Spirit is evidently meant. The perpetuity of that presence is guaranteed, "with you all the days"; and its time determined, "*unto the end of the age*." We are not saying that He will not be here after this period is finished; but we are saying that there is a distinct temporal mission of the Holy Spirit. And a full study confirms this. The present time is the dispensation of the Holy Spirit. The age-work He inaugurated on the day of Pentecost is now going on. It will continue until the Lord Jesus returns from heaven.

Then another order will be ushered in and another dispensational ministry succeed.

In *The Administration of the Holy Spirit in the Body of Christ*, Moberly divides the course of redemption so far accomplished into three stages: The first age, God the Father; the second age, God the Son; and the third age, God the Holy Spirit. This distribution seems to be correct, and so does his remark upon the inauguration of the last of these periods on the day of Pentecost. "At that moment," he says, "the third stage of the development [manifestation] of God for the restoration of the world finally began, never to come to an end or to be superseded on earth till the restitution of all things, when the Son of Man shall come again in the clouds of heaven, in like manner as his disciples saw him go into heaven." His coming will usher in "the age to come," whose powers have already been tasted by those who have been "made partakers of the Holy Spirit." For our purposes, then, we will concentrate on this present ministry of the Holy Spirit, whereby we secure our future.

"Therefore the Holy Ghost on this day—Pentecost—descended into the temple of his apostles, which he had prepared for himself, as a shower of sanctification, appearing no more as a transient visitor, but as a perpetual Comforter and as an eternal inhabitant. He came therefore on this day to his disciples, no longer by the grace of visitation and operation, but by the presence of his majesty."

—Augustine

2

The Advent of the Spirit

"For the Holy Ghost was not yet," is the surprising expression of John when speaking of "the Spirit which they that believe on him should receive" (John 7:39). Had not the Spirit been seen descending and remaining on Jesus like a dove at His baptism? Had He not been the divine agent in creation and in the illumination and inspiration of the patriarchs and prophets of the old dispensation? How then could John say that He "was not yet given"? The answer to this question provides the starting point for our study of the doctrine of the Spirit.

Augustine calls the day of Pentecost the "birthday" of the Holy Spirit for the same reason that we call the day when Mary brought forth her firstborn son "the birthday of Jesus Christ." Yet Jesus had existed "in the beginning with God." He was the agent in creation. By Him all things were. But on the day of His birth He became incarnate, that in the flesh He might fulfill His great ministry as the Apostle and High Priest of our confession, manifesting God to men and making himself an offering for the sins of the world. Not until after His birth in Bethlehem was Jesus in the world in His official capacity, in His divine ministry as mediator between man and God. In the same way not until after the day of Pentecost was the Holy Spirit in the world in His official office as mediator be-

tween men and Christ. In the following senses then is
Pentecost "the birthday of the Spirit":

1. The Holy Spirit, from that time on, took up His
residence on earth. The Christian Church throughout this
dispensation is the home of the Spirit as truly as heaven,
during this same period, is the home of Jesus Christ. This
is according to that sublime word of Jesus, called by one
"the highest promise which can be made to man": "If a
man love me, he will keep my words: and my Father will
love him, and we will come unto him, *and make our abode
with him*" (John 14:23). This promise was fulfilled at Pentecost. The first two Persons of the Godhead now hold residence in the church through the third. The Holy Spirit
during the present time is in office on earth, and all spiritual presence and divine communion of the Trinity with
men are through Him.

In other words, while the Father and the Son are visibly and personally in heaven, they are invisibly here in
the body of the faithful by the indwelling of the Comforter.
So that though we affirm that on the day of Pentecost the
Holy Spirit came to dwell on earth for this entire dispensation, we do not imply that He is no longer in heaven.
With God, unlike finite man, arrival in one place does not
necessitate withdrawal from another. Jesus uttered a saying concerning himself so mysterious and seemingly con-
tradictory that many have attempted to explain away its
literal and obvious meaning: "No man hath ascended up
to heaven but *he that came down from heaven, even the
Son of man who is in heaven*" (John 3:13). Christ on earth,
and yet in glory; here and there, at the same time, but
this is just like a thought that we embody in speech and
send forth from the mind. It still remains in the mind as
fully and distinctly as before it was expressed. Why should
this saying concerning our divine Lord seem incredible?
And as with the Son, so with the Spirit. The Holy Spirit
is on earth, abiding perpetually in the church. He is likewise in heaven in communion with the Father and the Son
from whom He proceeds. As coequal partner in the God-

head, He can never be separated from them any more than the sunbeam can be dissociated from the sun in which it has its source.

2. The Holy Spirit, in a mystical but very real sense, became embodied in the church on the day of Pentecost. Not that we would by any means put this embodiment on the same level as the incarnation of Jesus Christ. When "the Word was made flesh and dwelt among us," it was God entering into union with sinless humanity; here it is the Holy Spirit uniting himself with the church in its imperfect condition. Nevertheless, it is according to literal Scripture that the body of the faithful is indwelt by the divine Spirit. The fact is seen consistently throughout Scripture. "For he dwelleth with you and *shall be in you*" (John 14:17), said Jesus, speaking anticipatively of the coming of the Comforter. So truly was this prediction fulfilled that since the day of Pentecost the Holy Spirit is always spoken of as being in the church. "*If so be that the Spirit of God dwell in you*" (8:9) is the inspired assumption on which the deep teaching in Romans 8 proceeds. All the recognition and honor that the disciples paid to their Lord they now pay to the Holy Spirit, His true representative, His invisible self present in the body of believers. How simply and naturally this comes out in the findings of the first council at Jerusalem: "It seemed good *to the Holy Ghost and to us*" (Acts 15:28) runs the record, as though it had been said: "Peter and James and Barnabas and Saul and the rest were present, and also just as truly was the Holy Ghost."

When the first capital sin was committed in the church, the conspiracy and falsehood of Ananias and Sapphira, Peter's question is: "Why hath Satan filled thine heart to lie to the Holy Spirit?" "How is it that ye have agreed together to tempt the Spirit of the Lord?" (Acts 5:3, 9). Not only is the personal presence of the Spirit in the body of believers distinctly recognized, but He is there in authority and supremacy as the center of the assembly.

"Incarnated in the church!" do we say? We get this

conception by comparing the biblical characterizations of Christ and of the church. "This temple" was the name He gave to His own divine person, greatly to the scandal and indignation of the Jews. The evangelist explains to us that "he spoke of the temple of his body" (John 2:19, 21). A metaphor—a type—do we say? No! He said so because it was so. "The Word was made flesh and dwelt [tabernacled] among us, and we beheld his glory" (John 1:14). This is temple imagery. "Tabernacled" is the word used in Scripture for the dwelling of God with men, and the temple is God's dwelling place. The "glory" harmonizes with the same idea. As the Shechinah cloud rested above the mercy seat, the symbol and sign of God's presence, so from the Holy of Holies of our Lord's heart did the glory of God shine forth. "The glory as of the only begotten of the Father, full of grace and truth," certified Him to be the authentic temple of the Most High.

After His ascension and the sending down of the Spirit, the church takes the name her Lord had borne before. She is the temple of God, and the only temple that He has on earth during the present dispensation. "Know ye not that ye are the temple of God, and that the Spirit of God dwelleth in you?" asks the apostle (1 Cor. 3:16). This he speaks to the church in its corporate capacity. "A holy temple in the Lord, in whom ye also are *builded together* for a habitation of God through the Spirit," is the sublime description in the Epistle to the Ephesians (2:21, 22). We emphasize the fact that the same language is applied here to the church that Christ applies to himself. As with the Head, so with the mystical body. Each is indwelt by the Holy Spirit, and thus is God in some sense incarnated in both, and for the same reason. Christ was "the image of the invisible God" (Col. 1:15), and when He stood before men in the flesh, He could say to them, "He that hath seen me hath seen the Father" (John 14:9). It was only through the incarnation that the unknown God could become known and the unseen God become seen. So, after Christ had returned to the Father, and the world saw Him no more,

He sent the Paraclete to be incarnated in His body, the church. As the Father revealed himself through the Son, so the Son by the Holy Spirit now reveals himself through the church. As Christ was the image of the invisible God, so the church is appointed to be the image of the invisible Christ. His members, when they are glorified with Him, shall be the express image of His person.

This then is the mystery and the glory of this dispensation, not less true because mysterious, not less practical because glorious. In an admirable work on the Spirit, the distinction between the former and the present relation of the Spirit is thus stated: "In the old dispensation the Holy Spirit wrought *upon* believers, but did not in His person dwell in believers and abide permanently in them. He appeared unto men; He did not incarnate himself in man. His action was intermittent; He went and came like the dove which Noah sent forth from the ark, and which went to and fro, finding no rest; while in the new dispensation He dwells, He abides in the heart as the dove, His emblem, which John saw descending and alighting on the head of Jesus. Affianced of the soul, the Spirit went oft to see His betrothed, but was not yet one with her; the marriage was not consummated until the Pentecost, after the glorification of Jesus Christ."[1]

3. A still more obvious reason why before the day of Pentecost it could be said that "the Holy Ghost was not yet" is contained in the words, *"Because that Jesus was not yet glorified"* (John 7:39). In the order of the unfolding ages we see each of the persons of the Godhead exercising in turn an earthly ministry and dealing with man in the work of redemption. Under the law, God the Father comes down to earth and speaks to men from the cloud of Sinai and from the glory above the mercy seat. Under grace, God the Son is in the world, teaching, suffering, dying, and rising again. Under the dispensation now going on, the Holy Spirit is here carrying on the work of renewing

---

[1]"The Work of the Holy Spirit in Man," by Pastor Tophel, p. 32.

and sanctifying the church, the body of Christ.

There is a necessary succession in these divine ministries, both in time and in character. In the days of Moses it might have been said: "Christ is not yet," because the economy of God-Jehovah was not completed. The law first had to be given with its sacrifices and types and ceremonies and shadows. Man must be put on trial under the law until the appointed time of his schooling should be completed. *Then* must Christ come to fulfill all types and terminate all sacrifices in himself, to do for us "what the law could not do in that it was weak through the flesh" and to become "the end of the law for righteousness to every one that believeth." When in turn Christ had completed His redemptive work, *then* the Holy Ghost came down to communicate and make real to the church the finished work of Christ. In a word, as God the Son fulfills to men the work of God the Father, so God the Holy Spirit realizes to human hearts the work of God the Son.

There is a holy deference, if we may so say, between the Persons of the Trinity in regard to their respective ministries. When Christ was in office on earth, the Father commends us to Him, speaking from heaven and saying, "This is my beloved Son, hear ye him" (Matt. 17:5). When the Holy Spirit had entered upon His earthly office, Christ commends us to Him, speaking again from heaven with sevenfold reiteration, saying, "He that hath an ear, let him hear what *the Spirit* saith unto the churches" (Rev. 2:11). As each Person refers us to the teaching of the other, so in like manner does each in turn consummate the ministry of the other. Christ's words and works were not His own, but His Father's: "The words that I speak unto you I speak not of myself, but the Father that dwelleth in me he doeth the works" (John 14:10). The Spirit's teaching and communications are not His own, but Christ's: "Howbeit when he the Spirit of truth is come, he will guide you into all truth; *for he shall not speak of himself;* but whatsoever he shall hear that shall he speak; and he will show you things to come. *He shall glorify me; for he shall receive of mine and show it unto you"* (John 16:13, 14).

This order in the ministries of the Persons of the Godhead is so fixed and eternal that we find it distinctly foreshadowed even in the types of the Old Testament. Many speak slightingly of the types, but they are as accurate as mathematics. They fix the sequence of events in redemption as rigidly as the order of sunrise and sunset is fixed in the heavens. Nowhere in tabernacle or in temple shall we ever find the laver placed before the altar. The altar is Calvary and the laver is Pentecost. One stands for the sacrificial blood; the other, for the sanctifying Spirit. If any high priest were ignorantly to approach the brazen laver without first having come to the brazen altar, we might expect a rebuking voice to be heard from heaven: "Not yet the washing of water"; and such a saying would signify exactly the same as: "Not yet the Holy Ghost."

Again, when the leper was to be cleansed, observe that the blood was to be put upon the tip of his right ear, the thumb of his right hand, and the great toe of his right foot—*the oil upon the blood of the trespass offering* (Lev. 14). Never, we venture to say, in all the manifold repetitions of this divine ceremony, was this order once inverted so that the oil was first applied and then the blood. Interpreting type into antitype, this means that it was impossible that Pentecost could have preceded Calvary, or that the outpouring of the Spirit should have anticipated the shedding of the blood.

Not only was the order of these two great events of redemption fixed from the beginning, but their dates were marked in the calendar of typical time. The slaying of the paschal lamb told to generation after generation, though they did not realize it, the day of the year on which Christ our Passover should be sacrificed for us. The presentation of the wave sheaf before the Lord *"on the morrow after the Sabbath"* (Lev. 23:11–16) had for centuries fixed the time of our Lord's resurrection on the first day of the week. And the command to "count from the morrow after the Sabbath, from the day that ye brought the sheaf of the wave offering, *seven Sabbaths*," determined the day of Pentecost as the time of the descent of the Spirit. We sometimes think of the disciples waiting for an indefinite period in that upper room for the fulfillment of the promise of the Father, but the time had been fixed not only with God in eternity, but in the calendar of the Hebrew ritual upon earth. They tarried in prayer for ten days simply because after the forty days of the Lord's sojourn on earth subsequent to His resurrection, ten days remained of the "seven Sabbaths" period.

To sum up what we are saying: The Spirit of God is the successor of the Son of God in His official ministry on earth. Until Christ's earthly work for His church had been finished, the Spirit's work in this world could not properly begin. The office of the Holy Spirit is to communicate Christ to us—Christ in His entirety. Our Savior's redemptive work was not complete when He died on the cross, or when He rose from the dead, or even when He ascended. Not until He sat down in His Father's throne, summing up all His ministry in himself—"I am He that liveth and was dead, and behold I am alive forevermore"—did the full Christ stand ready to be communicated to His church.[2] By the first Adam's sin, God's communion with man through the Holy Spirit was broken, and their union ruptured. When the second Adam came up from His cross and resurrection and took His place at God's right hand, there was a restoration of this broken fellowship. Very beautiful are the words of our risen Lord bearing on this point: "I ascend to my Father and your Father, to my God and your God" (John 20:17). The place the divine Son had won for

---

[2]"Christ having reached his goal, and not till then, bequeathes to his followers the graces that invested his earthly course; the ascending Elijah leaves his mantle behind him. It is only an extension of the same principle, that the declared office of the Holy Spirit being to complete the image of Christ in every faithful follower by effecting in this world a spiritual death and resurrection—a point attested in every epistle—*the image could not be stamped until the reality had been wholly accomplished; the Divine Artist could not fitly descend to make the copy before the entire original had been provided.*"—Archer Butler

himself in the Father's heart He had won for us also. All of the acceptance and standing and privilege that was now His was ours too by redemptive right, and the Holy Spirit is sent down to confirm and realize in us what Christ had won for us. Without the expiatory work of Christ for us, the sanctifying work of the Spirit in us was impossible. And on the other hand, without the work of the Spirit within us, the work of Christ for us was to no benefit.

"And when the day of Pentecost was fully come" (Acts 2:1). What these words mean historically, typically, and doctrinally, we are now prepared to understand. The true wave sheaf had been presented in the temple on high. Christ the firstfruits, brought from the grave on "the morrow after the Sabbath," or the first day of the week, now stands before God accepted on our behalf. The seven Sabbaths from the resurrection day have been counted, and Pentecost has come. Then suddenly, to those who were "all of one accord in one place . . . there came a sound from heaven as of a rushing mighty wind, and it filled all the house where they were sitting, and there appeared unto them cloven tongues, like as of fire, and sat upon each of them, and they were all filled with the Holy Ghost" (Acts 2:1–4). As the manger of Bethlehem was the cradle of the Son of God, so was the upper room the cradle of the Spirit of God. As the advent of "the Holy Child" was a testimony that God had "visited and redeemed His people," so was the coming of the Holy Spirit. The fact that the Comforter is here is proof that the Advocate is there in the presence of the Father. Boldly Peter and the other apostles now confront the rulers with their testimony: "Whom ye slew and hanged on a tree . . . Him hath God exalted with his right hand to be a prince and a Saviour, to give repentance to Israel and forgiveness of sins; and we are his witnesses of these things; *and so also is the Holy Ghost, whom God hath given to them that obey him*" (Acts 5:30–32). As the sound of the golden bells upon the high priest's garments within the Holiest gave evidence that he was alive, so the sound of the Holy Spirit proceeding from heaven and heard

in that upper chamber was an incontestable witness that the great High Priest whom they had just seen passing through the cloud-curtain, entering within the veil, was still living for them in the presence of the Father. Thus the "birthday" of the Holy Spirit came and the events of His earthly mission will now be considered in their order.

"The name Paraclete is applied to Christ as well as to the Spirit; and properly: For it is the common office of each to console and encourage us and to preserve us by their defense. Christ was their [the disciples'] patron so long as he lived in the world; he then committed them to the guidance and protection of the Spirit. If any one asks us whether we are not under the guidance of Christ, the answer is easy: Christ is a perpetual guardian, but not visibly. As long as he walked on the earth he appeared openly as their guardian: now he preserves us by his Spirit. He calls the Spirit 'another Comforter,' in view of the distinction which we observe in the blessings proceeding from each."

—John Calvin

3

The Naming of the Spirit

The Son of God was named by the angel before He was conceived in the womb: "Thou shalt call his name Jesus: for he shall save his people from their sins" (Matt. 1:21). Thus He came, not to receive a name, but to fulfill a name already predetermined for Him. In like manner, the Holy Spirit was named by our Lord before His advent into the world: "But when the Comforter [Paraclete] is come, whom I will send unto you from the Father..." (John 15:26). This designation of the Holy Spirit occurs here for the first time—a new name for the new ministry that He is about to enter.

The reader will find in almost any critical commentary discussions of the meaning of the word and its correct translation, whether by "Comforter," "Advocate," "Teacher," or "Helper." But the question cannot be fully settled by an appeal to classical or patristic Greek, because, we believe, it is a divinely given name whose real significance must be made manifest in the actual life and history of the Spirit. The name is the person himself, and only as we know the person can we interpret His name. Why attempt then to translate this word any more than we do the name of Jesus? We might well transfer it into our English version, leaving the history of the church from the Acts of the Apostles to the experience of the latest saint to fill into it the great significance which it was intended to contain. It is certain that the language of the Holy Spirit can never be fully understood by an appeal to the lexicon. The heart of the church is the best dictionary of the Spirit. While all the before-mentioned synonyms are correct, neither one nor all together is sufficient to bring out the full significance of the great name, "The Paraclete."

Let us consider, however, how much is suggested by the literal meaning *Paracletos* and by all that our Lord says concerning Him in His last discourse. "To call to one's aid" is the meaning of the verb from which the name is derived. Very beautiful, therefore, is the word in its application to the disciples at the time the Spirit was given. They had lost the visible presence of their Lord. The sorrow of His removal from them through the cross and the sepulcher had after three days been turned into joy by His resurrection. But now another separation had come, His departure to the Father after the cloud had received Him out of sight. In this last and longer bereavement, what should they do? Their beloved Master had told them beforehand what to do. They were to call upon the Father to send them One to fill the vacant place, and He who should be sent would be the "Paraclete," the "one called to their help."

But what deep questionings must have arisen in their hearts as they heard the Savior's promise: "If I go not away, the Comforter [Paraclete] will not come unto you; but if I depart, I will send him unto you." Did they begin to ask whether the mysterious comer would be a "person"? Impossible to imagine. For He was to take the place of that greatest of persons, to do for them even greater things than He had done and to lead them into even larger knowledge than He had imparted. The discussion of the personality of the Holy Spirit is so unnatural in the light of Christ's last discourse that we studiously avoid it. Let us treat the question, therefore, from the point of view of Christ's own words and try to put ourselves under the impression which they make upon us. To state the matter as simply as possible: Jesus is about to vacate His office on earth as teacher and prophet, but before doing so He would introduce us to His successor. In this paschal discourse Jesus aims to acquaint us with the mysterious, invisible coming personage whom He names the "Paraclete" by comparing Him with himself, the known and the visible one. Examining His comparisons, we may find in them several groups of seeming contradictions, and just such contradictions as we should expect if this comer is indeed a person of the Godhead. Of the coming Paraclete then we find these intimations.[1]

1. He is another, yet the same: "And I will pray the Father, and he shall give you another Comforter" (John 14:16). By the use of the expression *"another,"* our Lord distinguishes the Paraclete from himself, but He also puts Him on the same plane with himself. For there is no equality or even comparison between a person and an influence. If the promised visitor were to be only an impersonal emanation from God, it would seem impossible that our Lord should have so associated Him with himself as to say, "I go to be an Advocate for you in heaven (1 John 2:1), and I send another to be an Advocate for you on earth."

But if Christ thus distinguishes the Comforter from himself, He also identifies Him with himself: "I will not leave you comfortless: *I will come to you*" (John 14:18). By common consent this promise refers to the advent of the Spirit, which the connection plainly indicates. And yet almost in the same breath He says, "The Comforter, which is the Holy Ghost, whom the Father will send in my Name . . ." (John 14:26). Our Lord makes the same event to be at once His coming and His sending, and He speaks

---

[1]The most obvious reason for concluding that the Holy Spirit is a person is that He performs actions and stands in relations which belong only to a person, e.g.: He speaks (Acts 1:16); He works miracles (Acts 2:4; 8:39); He sets ministers over churches (Acts 20:28); He commands and forbids (Acts 8:29; 11:12; 13:2; 16:6, 7); He prays for us (Rom. 8:26); He witnesses (Rom. 8:16); He can be grieved (Eph. 4:30); He can be blasphemed (Mark 3:29); He can be resisted (Acts 7:51).

of the Spirit both as His own presence and as His substitute during His absence. So we must conclude that the Paraclete is Christ's other self, a third Person in that blessed Trinity, of which He is the second.

2. The Paraclete is subordinate yet superior in His ministry to the church. "For he shall not speak of himself; but whatsoever he shall hear, that shall he speak. . . . He shall glorify me; for he shall receive of mine, and shall show it unto you" (John 16:13, 14).

Here we mark the holy deference between the Persons of the Trinity. Each receives from another what He communicates, and each magnifies another in His praises. As Bengel concisely states it, "The Son glorifies the Father; the Spirit glorifies the Son." What then is the office of the Holy Spirit but that of communicating and applying the work of Christ to human hearts? If He convinces of sin, it is by exhibiting the gracious redemptive work of the Savior and showing men their guilt in not believing on Him. If He witnesses to the penitent of His acceptance, it is by testifying of the atoning blood of Jesus in which that acceptance is grounded. If He regenerates and sanctifies the heart, it is by communicating to it the life of the risen Lord. Christ is "all" in himself, and through the Spirit "in all" those whom the Spirit renews. This reverent subjection of the earthly Comforter to the heavenly Christ contains a deep lesson for those who are indwelt by the Spirit, making them rejoice to be witnesses rather than originators.

With this subordination of the Holy Spirit to Christ, how is it yet true that such a great advantage was to be gained for the church by the departure of the Savior and the consequent advent of the Spirit to take His place? That it would be so is what is plainly affirmed in the following text: "It is expedient for you that I go away: for if I go not away, the Comforter will not come unto you; but if I depart, I will send him unto you" (John 16:7). If the Spirit is simply the measure of the Son, His sole work being to communicate the work of the Son, what gain could there be in Christ's departure in order for the Spirit to come. Would it not be simply the exchange of His visible presence for His invisible?

The answer to this question is obvious. It was not the earthly Christ whom the Holy Spirit was to communicate to the church, but the heavenly Christ—the Christ reinvested with His eternal power, reclothed with the glory He had with the Father before the world was, and reendowed with the infinite treasures of grace He had purchased by His death on the cross. It is as though—to use a very inadequate illustration—a beloved father were to say to his family: "My children, I have provided well for your needs; but your condition is one of poverty compared with what it may become. By the death of a relative in my home country, I have become heir to an immense estate. If you will only submit cheerfully to my leaving you and crossing the sea, and entering into my inheritance, I will send you back a thousand times more than you could have by my remaining with you." Only in the instance we are considering, Christ is the One who leaves the inheritance as well as the heir. By His death the inheritance becomes available, and when He had ascended into heaven, He sent down the Holy Spirit to distribute the estate among those who were joint heirs with Him.

What this estate is may be best summarized in two beautiful expressions of frequent recurrence in the epistles of Paul: "The riches of his grace" (Eph. 1:7), and "The riches of his glory" (Eph. 3:16). On the cross "the riches of his grace" was secured to us in the forgiveness of sins. On the throne "the riches of his glory" was secured to us in our being strengthened with all might by His Spirit in the inner man—in the indwelling of Christ in our hearts by faith and in our infilling with all the fullness of God. The divine wealth only becomes completely available on the death, resurrection, and ascension of our Lord, so that the Holy Spirit, the divine Supplier, had not the full inheritance to convey till Jesus was glorified.

Observe, therefore, in the farewell discourse of our Lord,

the frequent recurrence of the words: *"Because I go to the Father,"* one of the sayings that greatly perplexed His disciples. In the light of all that Jesus says in this connection, let us see if its meaning becomes clear to us. "If ye loved me, ye would rejoice, because I said, I go unto the Father: for my Father is greater than I" (John 14:28), He says in the same connection. We cannot here enter into the deep question of the *kenosis*, or self-emptying, of the Son of God in His incarnation. It is enough that we follow the plain teaching of the Scripture, that though "being in the form of God, thought it not robbery to be equal with God; but made himself of no reputation, and took upon him the form of a servant" (Phil. 2:6, 7). What now does His going to the Father signify but a refilling with that of which He had been emptied concerning His coequality with God? The greater blessing which He could confer upon His church by His departure seems to lie in the fact of the greater power and glory into which He would enter by His enthronement at God's right hand. As Luther pointedly puts it: "Therefore do I go, he saith, where I shall be greater than I now am, that is, to the Father, and it is better that I shall pass out of this obscurity and weakness into the power and glory in which the Father is."

In the light of this interpretation, the meaning of our Lord's words above quoted does not seem difficult. The Paraclete was to communicate Christ to His church—His life, His power, His riches, His glory. In His exaltation all these were to be very greatly increased. "All things that the Father hath are mine" (John 16:15), He says. And though He had for a time voluntarily disinherited himself of His heavenly possessions, He is now to be repossessed of them. "Therefore said I, that he shall take of mine, and shall show it unto you" (16:15). Christ at God's right hand will have more to give than while on earth; therefore the church will have more to receive through the Paraclete than through the visible Christ.

What obvious significance then do the following sayings from this farewell sermon of Jesus have: "Verily, verily, I say unto you, He that believeth on me, the works that I do shall he do also; and greater works than these shall he do; *because I go unto my Father*" (John 14:12). The earthly Christ is equal only to himself thus conditioned, and if the Holy Spirit shall communicate His power to His disciples, they will do the same works that He does. But the heavenly Christ is coequal with the Father; therefore, when He shall ascend to the Father and the Spirit shall take of His and communicate it to His church, she will do greater works than these. The stream of life, in other words, will have greater power because of the higher source from which it proceeds. Very deep are the mysteries here considered, and we can speak of them only in the light which we get by comparing scripture with scripture. Did the risen Christ breathe on His disciples and say to them, "Receive ye the Holy Ghost"?[2] "It is enough, Lord, that we have received the Spirit from thee," they might well have said. Yet it was not enough for Him to give. For looking on to the day of His enthronement, He says, "But when the Comforter is come, whom I will send unto you from the Father, even the Spirit of truth, which proceedeth from the Father, he shall testify of me" (John 15:26). When Jesus has ascended "on high," then can the Holy Spirit communicate "the power from on high." Therefore, it is expedient that He go away.

As with the power which Christ was to impart to His church through the Paraclete, so with the righteousness which He was both to impute and to impart: Its highest source must be found in heaven. "And when he [the Comforter] is come, he will reprove the world . . . of righteousness, *because I go to my Father*, and ye see me no more" (John 16:8–10). We may truly say that the righteousness of Christ was not completely finished and authenticated till He sat down at the right hand of the majesty on high. By His death He perfectly satisfied the claims of a violated

---

[2]Let it be observed that in this communication of the risen Christ it is not said, "Receive ye *the* Holy Ghost"—the article being significantly omitted in the Greek (John 20:22).

law, but this fact was not attested until the grave gave
back the certificate of discharge in His released and risen
body. By His resurrection He was "declared to be the Son
of God with power, according to the Spirit of holiness"
(Rom. 1:4). But the fact was not fully verified till God had
"set him at his own right hand in the heavenly places, far
above all principality, and power, and might, and dominion, and every name that is named" (Eph. 1:20, 21). Now
in His consummated glory He is prepared to be "made
unto us wisdom, and righteousness, and sanctification, and
redemption" (1 Cor. 1:30). He who had been "manifest in
the flesh" that He might be made sin for us was now "justified in the Spirit" and "received up into glory" (1 Tim.
3:16) that He might be made righteousness to us, and that
"we might be made the righteousness of God in him" (2
Cor. 5:21). Christ's coronation, in a word, is the indispensable condition for our justification. Till He who was
made a curse for us is crowned with glory and honor, we
cannot be assured of our acceptance with the Father. How
deep the current of thought which flows through this narrow channel: "Because I go to the Father."

3. The Paraclete teaches only the things of Christ, yet
teaches more than Christ taught: "I have yet many things
to say unto you, but ye cannot bear them now. Howbeit
when he, the Spirit of truth, is come, he will guide you
into all truth" (John 16:12, 13). It is as though He had
said, "I have brought you a little way in the knowledge of
my doctrine; He shall bring you all the way." One reason
for this seems plain: The teaching of Jesus during His
earthly ministry waited to be illumined by a light not
risen—the light of the cross, the light of the sepulcher, the
light of the ascension. Therefore until these events had
come to pass, Christian doctrine was undeveloped, and
could not be fully communicated to the disciples.

But this is not all. The "because I go to the Father"
still gives the key to our Lord's meaning. "But whatsoever
he shall hear, that shall he speak: and he will show you
things to come" (John 16:13). Very wonderful is this hint

of the mutual converse of the Godhead, so that the Paraclete is described as listening while He leads, as having
an ear in heaven attentive to the Father and the glorified
Son, while He extends an unseen guidance to the flock on
earth, communicating to them what He has heard from
the Father and the Son. And we may reverently ask, Has
not the glorified Christ more of knowledge and revelation
to communicate than He had in the days of His humiliation? Of "the things to come," has He not secrets to impart
which hitherto may have been hidden in the counsels of
the Father? Taking a single illustration from the words of
Christ concerning His second advent, He says, "But of that
day and that hour knoweth no man, no, not the angels
which are in heaven, neither the Son, but the Father"
(Mark 13:32[3]). It is best that we should interpret these
words frankly and not say, as some do, that He did not
know only in the sense that He was not permitted to dis-
close. We should rather admit it possible that while in His
humiliation and under the veil of His incarnation, this
secret was hidden from His eyes.

But is it not presumptuous for us to conclude, therefore, that He does not even *now* know the day of His coming? How constantly that text is quoted as a decisive and
final prohibition of all inquiry into the nearness of our
Lord's return in glory. Have we forgotten that since our
Lord ascended to the Father, He has given us a further
revelation, that wondrous book of Revelation? And one
characteristic feature of this book is its chronological pre-
dictions concerning the time of the end, its mystical dates,
which have led many to inquire diligently "what manner
of time" the Spirit did signify in giving us these markers.
This being so, we may ask, If we are not irreverent in
concluding with many devout expositors that our Savior
meant what He said in declaring that He did "not yet"
know the time of His advent, are we presumptuous in tak-

---

[3]"Neither the Son": "It is more than *neither*; it is *not yet the Son*," says
Morrison the commentator.

ing literally the opening words of Revelation? "The Revelation of Jesus Christ, which God gave unto him, to show unto his servants the things which must shortly come to pass." It was because of His going unto the Father that greater works and greater riches were to attend the church after Pentecost. Why may we not assign to the same cause also the fuller revelation of the future and the leading into more complete truth concerning the blessed hope of the church? In other words, if we may think of Christ as entering into larger revelation as He returns to the glory which He had with the Father, must we not think of larger communications of truth by the blessed Paraclete?

We have truly learned something of the nature and offices of the Spirit by this study of His new name and the discourse in which the Lord introduces Him to His disciples. At least the study should enable us to distinguish two inspired terms that have been needlessly confused by many writers, namely, the words *"Paraclete"* and *"Parousia."* The latter word, which constantly occurs in Scripture as describing our Lord's second coming, has been applied in several learned works to the advent of the Holy Spirit. And since Christ came in the person of the Spirit, it has been argued that the Redeemer's promised advent in glory has already taken place. But this is to confuse terms whose use in Scripture marks them as clearly distinct. Observe their difference: In the Paraclete, Christ comes spiritually and invisibly; in the Parousia, He comes bodily and gloriously. The advent of the Paraclete is really conditioned on the Savior's personal departure from His people: "If I go not away, the Comforter will not come to you" (John 16:7). The Parousia, on the other hand, is realized only in His personal return to His people: "For what is our hope or joy or crown of rejoicing? Are not even ye in the *presence* of our Lord Jesus Christ *at his coming*?" (1 Thess. 2:19). The Paraclete attends the church in the days of her humiliation. The Parousia introduces the church into the day of her glory. In the Paraclete, Christ came to dwell with the church on earth: "I will not leave you comfortless; I will come to you" (John 14:18). In the Parousia, Christ comes to take the church to dwell with himself in glory: "I will come again, and receive you unto myself; that where I am, there ye may be also" (John 14:3). Christ prayed on behalf of His bereaved church for the coming of this Paraclete: "And I will pray the Father and he shall give you another Comforter" (John 14:16). The Holy Spirit now prays with the pilgrim-church for the hastening of the Parousia: "And the Spirit and the bride say, Come" (Rev. 22:17). These two can be understood only in their mutual relations. Christ, who gave the new name to the Holy Spirit, can best interpret that name to us by making us acquainted with himself. May that name be for us so real a symbol of personal presence that while we are strangers and pilgrims on the earth, we may walk evermore "in the *paraclesis* of the Holy Ghost" (Acts 9:31).

"But now the Holy Ghost is given more perfectly, for he is no longer present by his operation as of old, but is present with us so to speak, and converses with us in a substantial manner. For it was fitting that, as the Son had conversed with us in the body, the spirit should also come among us in a bodily manner."

—Gregory Nazianzen

4

The Embodying of the Spirit

"The church, which is Christ's body," began its history and development at Pentecost. Believers had been saved and the influences of the Spirit had been manifested to men from Adam to Christ. But now an *ecclesia*, an out-gathering, was to be made to constitute the mystical body of Christ, incorporated into Him the Head and indwelt by Him through the Holy Spirit. The definition that a church is "a voluntary association of believers, united together for the purposes of worship and edification," is most inadequate, not to say incorrect. This is no more true than the idea that hands and feet and eyes and ears are voluntarily united in the human body for the purposes of locomotion and work. The church is formed from within— Christ present by the Holy Spirit, regenerating men by the action of the Spirit and organizing them into himself as the living center. The Head and the body are therefore one and predestined to the same history of humiliation and glory.

And as they are one in fact, so are they one in name. He whom God anointed and filled with the Holy Spirit is called "the Christ," and the church, which is His body and fullness, is also called "the Christ." "For as the body is one, and hath many members, and all the members of that one body, being many, are one body: *so also is Christ*" (1

Cor. 12:12). Here plainly and with wondrous honor the church is named *the Christ*. Bishop Andrews comments on this fact beautifully, saying, "Christ is both in heaven and on earth; as he is called the Head of his church, he is in heaven; but in respect of his body which is called Christ, he is on earth."

When the Holy Spirit was sent down from heaven, this great work of His embodying began, and it is to continue until the end of the age. Christ, if we may say it reverently, became mystically a babe again on the day of Pentecost, and the hundred and twenty were His infantile body, as once more through the Holy Spirit He incarnated himself in His flesh. Now He is growing and increasing in His members, and so will He continue to do "till we all come in the unity of the faith and of the knowledge of the Son of God, unto a perfect man, unto the measure of the stature of fulness of Christ" (Eph. 4:13). Then the Christ on earth will be taken up into visible union with the Christ in heaven, and the Head and the body be glorified together.

Observe how the history of the church's formation, as recorded in the Acts, harmonizes with this thought. The story of Pentecost culminates in the words, "and the same day there were added about three thousand souls" (Acts 2:41). We naturally ask, added to whom? The King James translators have answered our question by inserting in italics "to them." But not so speaks the Holy Spirit. And when, a few verses further on in the same chapter, we read, "And the Lord added to the church daily such as should be saved," we need to be reminded that the words "to the church" are spurious. All such glosses and interpolations have only tended to mar the sublime teaching of this first chapter of the Holy Spirit's history. "And believers were the more added *to the Lord*" (Acts 5:14). "And much people was added *unto the Lord*" (Acts 11:24). This is the language of inspiration—not the mutual union of believers, but their divine co-uniting with Christ; not voluntary association of Christians, but their sovereign incorporation into the Head and this incorporation effected by the Head through the Holy Spirit.

If we ask concerning the way of admission into this divine *ecclesia*, the teaching of Scripture is explicit: "For by one Spirit are we all baptized into one body" (1 Cor. 12:13). The baptism in water marks the formal introduction of the believer into the church. But this is the symbol, not the substance. For observe the identity of form between the ritual and the spiritual. "I indeed baptize you in water. . . ," said John, "but he that cometh after me . . . shall baptize you in the Holy Ghost and in fire" (Matt. 3:11). As in the one instance the disciple was submerged in the element of water, so in the other he was to be submerged in the element of the Spirit. And thus it was in actual historic fact. The upper room became the Spirit's baptistery, if we may use the figure. His presence "filled all the house where they were sitting," and "they were all filled with the Holy Ghost." The baptistery would never need to be refilled, for Pentecost was once and for all, and the Spirit then came to abide in the church perpetually. But each believer throughout the age would need to be infilled with the Spirit that dwells in the body of Christ. In other words, it seems clear that the baptism of the Spirit was given once for the whole church, extending from Pentecost to Parousia. "There is one Lord, one faith, one baptism" (Eph. 4:5). As there is "one body" reaching through the entire dispensation, so there is "one baptism" for that body given on the day of Pentecost. Thus if we rightly understand the meaning of Scripture it is true that both in time and fact "in one Spirit we were all baptized into one body, whether Jews or Greeks, whether bond or free."

The typical foreshadowing, as seen in the church in the wilderness, is very suggestive at this point: "Moreover, brethren, I would not that ye should be ignorant, how that all our fathers were under the cloud and all passed through the sea; and were all baptized unto Moses in the cloud and in the sea" (1 Cor. 10:1). They were baptized *into* Moses by their passage through the sea, identified with him as their leader, and committed to him in corporate fellowship. Even so were they also baptized into Jehovah, who in the cloud of glory now took His place in the midst of the camp and tabernacled henceforth with them. The type is perfect as all inspired types are. The antitype first appears in Christ our Lord, baptized in water at the Jordan and then baptized in the Holy Spirit, who "descended from heaven like a dove and abode upon him." Then it recurred again in the waiting disciples, who besides the baptism of water, which had doubtless already been received, now were baptized "in the Holy Ghost and in fire." Henceforth they were in the divine element, as their fathers had been in the wilderness, "not in the flesh, but *in the Spirit*" (Rom. 8:9), called "to live according to God *in the Spirit*" (1 Pet. 4:6), to "walk *in the Spirit*" (Gal. 5:25), "praying always with all prayer and supplication *in the Spirit*" (Eph. 6:18). In a word, on the day of Pentecost the entire body of Christ was baptized into the element and presence of the Holy Spirit as a permanent condition. And though one might object that the body as a whole was not yet in existence, we reply that neither was the complete church in existence when Christ died on Calvary, yet all believers are repeatedly said to have died with Him.

To change the figure of baptism for a moment to another that is used synonymously, that of the anointing of the Spirit, we have in Exodus a beautiful typical illustration of our thought. At Aaron's consecration the precious ointment was not only poured upon his head but ran down in rich profusion upon his body and upon his priestly garments. This fact is taken up by the psalmist when he sings, "Behold, how good and how pleasant it is for brethren to dwell together in unity! It is like the precious ointment upon the head that ran down Aaron's beard, down to the skirts of his garments" (Ps. 133:1, 2). Of Christ, our great High Priest, we read: "How God anointed Jesus of Nazareth with the Holy Ghost and with power" (Acts 10:38). But it was not for himself alone but also for His brethren that He obtained this holy unction. He received that He might communicate. "Upon whom thou shalt see the Spirit descending and remaining on him, the same is he which baptizeth in the Holy Ghost" (John 1:33). And now we behold our Aaron, our great High Priest, who has passed through the heavens, Jesus the Son of God, standing in the holiest in heaven. "Thou didst love righteousness and hated iniquity" is the divine tribute now passed upon Him; "therefore God, thy God, hath anointed thee with the oil of gladness above thy fellows" (Heb. 1:9). He, the *Christos*, the Anointed, stands above and for the *Christoi*, His anointed brethren, and on the day of Pentecost the unction of the Holy Spirit poured from Him, the Head, in rich profusion upon His mystical body. It has been flowing down ever since and will continue to flow until the last member shall have been incorporated with himself, and so anointed by the one Spirit into the one body, which is the church.

It is true that in one instance subsequent to Pentecost, the baptism in the Holy Ghost is spoken of. When the Spirit fell on the house of Cornelius, Peter is reminded of the Lord's word: "John indeed baptized in water, but ye shall be baptized in the Holy Ghost" (Acts 11:16). This was a great crisis in the history of the church, the opening of the door of faith to the Gentiles, and it would seem that these new subjects of grace now came into participation of an already present Spirit. Yet Pentecost still appears to have been the age-baptism of the church. As Calvary was once for all, so was the visitation of the upper room.

Consider now that, as through the Holy Spirit we become incorporated into the body of Christ, we are in the same way assimilated to the Head of that body, which is Christ. What, to the angels and principalities who gaze evermore upon the face of Jesus, must be the sight of an unholy and misshapen church on earth, standing in that place of honor called "his body." An unsanctified church dishonors the Lord, especially by its inconsistency. A noble head, lofty-browed and intellectual, upon a deformed and stunted body is a pitiable sight. Of the early church, Professor Harnack says, *"Originally the church was the heavenly bride of Christ, and the abiding place of the Holy Spirit."*

Let the reader consider how much is involved in this definition. Watching for the return of the Bridegroom induces holiness of life and conduct in the bride. The supreme work of the Spirit is directed to this end, that "he may establish your hearts unblameable in holiness before God, even our Father, at the coming of our Lord Jesus Christ with all his saints" (1 Thess. 3:13). In accomplishing this end, He effects all other and subordinate ends. The glorified Christ manifests himself to man through His body.

If there is a perfect correspondence between himself and His members, then there will be a true manifestation of himself to the world.[1] Therefore does the Spirit abide in the body that the body may be "inChristed," indwelt by Christ and transfigured into the likeness of Christ. Only thus, as "a chosen generation, a royal priesthood, a holy nation, a peculiar people," can it "shew forth the praises of him who hath called you out of darkness into his marvelous light" (1 Pet. 2:9). And who is the Christ that is thus to be manifested? From the throne He gives us His name: "I am he that liveth and was dead, and behold, I am alive for evermore" (Rev. 1:18). Christ in glory is not simply what He is, but what He was and what He is to be. As a tree gathers up into itself all the growths of former years and contains them in its trunk, so Jesus on the throne is all that He was and is and is to be. In other words, His death as well as His life is a perpetual fact.

And His church is predestined to be like Him in death and life. It not only receives its headship in Him that it "may grow up into him in all things, which is the Head, even Christ," but also builds itself upward from Him, "from whom the whole body, fitly joined together and compacted by that which every joint supplieth . . . maketh increase

---

[1]"The Holy Spirit not only dwells in the church as his habitation, but also uses her as the living organism whereby he moves and walks forth in the world, and speaks to the world and acts upon the world. He is the soul of the church which is Christ's body."—Bishop Webb, The Presence and Office of the Spirit, p. 47.

of the body" (Eph. 4:15, 16). If the church will literally manifest Christ, then she must be both a living and a dying church. To this she is committed in the divinely given form of her baptism. "Know ye not, that so many of us as were baptized into Jesus Christ were baptized into his death; therefore we were buried with him by baptism into death: that like as Christ was raised up from the dead by the glory of the Father, even so we also should walk in newness of life" (Rom. 6:3, 4). And the baptism of the Holy Spirit into which we have been brought is designed to accomplish inwardly and spiritually what the baptism of water foreshadows outwardly and typically: reproduction in us of the life and death of our Lord.

First, His life in His members. "For the law of the Spirit of life in Christ Jesus hath made me free from the law of sin and death" (Rom. 8:2). That is, that which has been the actuating principle within us—sin and death— is now to be met and mastered by another principle, the law of life, of which the Holy Spirit is the author and sustainer. As by our natural spirit we are united with the first Adam and partakers of his falleness, so by the Holy Spirit we are now united with the second Adam and par- take of His glorified nature. To energize the body of Christ by maintaining its identity with the risen Head is, in a word, the unceasing work of the Holy Spirit.

Second, His death in His members. This principle is to be constantly effected by the indwelling Spirit. The church, which is "the fullness of him that filleth all in all," com- pletes in the world His crucifixion as well as His resur- rection. This is certainly Paul's profound thought when he speaks of filling up "that which is behind of the afflic- tions of Christ in my flesh, for his body's sake, which is the church" (Col. 1:24). In other words, the church, as the complement of her Lord, must have a life experience and a death experience running parallel.

It is remarkable how exact is this figure of the body, which is employed to symbolize the church. In the human system, life and death are constantly working together. A certain amount of tissue must die every day and be cast out and buried, and a certain amount of new tissue must also be created and nourished daily in the same body. Arrest the death process and it is just as certain to produce disorder as though you were to arrest the life process. This is true of the corporate body also. The church must die daily in fulfillment of the crucified life of her Head, as well as live daily in the manifestation of His glorified life. This italicized sentence from a recent book is worthy to be made a golden text for Christians: *"The Church is Christian no more than as it is the organ of the continuous passion of Christ."* To sympathize, in the literal sense of suffering with our sinning and lost humanity, is not only the duty of the church but the absolutely essential condition for her true manifestation of her Lord. A self-indulgent church disfigures Christ, a covetous church bears false witness against Christ, and a worldly church betrays Christ, giving Him over once more to be mocked and reviled by His enemies.

The resurrection of our Lord is prolonged in His body, as we see plainly. Every regeneration is a pulse beat of His throne life. But too little do we recognize the fact that His crucifixion must be prolonged side by side with His resurrection. "If any man will come after me, let him deny himself, and take up his cross, and follow me." The church is called to live a glorified life in communion with her Head and a crucified life in her contact with the world. And the Holy Spirit dwells evermore in the church to effect this twofold manifestation of Christ. "But God be thanked, that ye . . . have obeyed from the heart that form of doctrine which was delivered you," writes the Apostle (Rom. 6:17). The pattern, as the context shows, is Christ dead and risen. If the church truly lives in the Spirit, He will keep her so malleable that she will obey this divine mold just as metal conforms to the die in which it is struck. If she yields to the sway of "the spirit that now worketh in the children of disobedience," she will be stereotyped according to the fashion of the world, and they that look upon her will fail to see Christ in her.

"To the disciples, the baptism of the Spirit was very distinctly not his first bestowal for regeneration, but the definite communication of his presence in power of their glorified Lord. Just as there was a twofold operation of the one Spirit in the Old and New Testaments, of which the state of the disciples before and after Pentecost was the striking illustration, so there may be, and in the great majority of Christians is, a corresponding difference of experience. . . . When once the distinct recognition of what the indwelling of the Spirit was meant to bring is brought home to the soul, and it is ready to give up all to be made partaker of it, the believer may ask and expect what may be termed a baptism of the Spirit. Praying to the Father in accordance to the two prayers in Ephesians, and coming to Jesus in the renewed surrender of faith and obedience, he may receive such an inflow of the Holy Spirit as shall consciously lift him to a different level from the one on which he has hitherto lived."

—Rev. Andrew Murray

5

The Enduement of the Spirit

We have maintained in the previous chapter that the baptism in the Holy Spirit was given once for all on the day of Pentecost, when the Paraclete came in person to make His abode in the church. But, that does not mean that every believer has received this baptism. God's gift is one thing; our appropriation of that gift is quite another. Our relation to the second and to the third Persons of the Godhead is exactly parallel in this respect. "God so loved the world that he *gave* his only begotten Son" (John 3:16). "But as many as *received him*, to them gave he power to become the sons of God, even to them that believe on his name" (John 1:12). Here are the two sides of salvation, the divine and the human, which are absolutely coessential.

The doctrine of universalism maintains that since God gave His Son to the world, all the world has the Son, consciously or unconsciously, and therefore all the world will be saved. It need not be said that a true evangelical teaching must reject this theory as utterly untenable, since it ignores the necessity of individual faith in Christ. But some orthodox writers have urged an almost identical view with respect to the Holy Spirit. They have contended that the enduement of the Spirit is "not any special or more advanced experience, but simply the condition of everyone who is a child of God," that "believers converted after Pentecost, and living in other localities, are just as really endowed with the indwelling Spirit as those who actually partook of the Pentecostal blessing at Jerusalem."[1]

On the contrary, it seems clear from the Scriptures that it is still the duty and privilege of believers to receive the Holy Spirit by a conscious, definite act of appropriating faith, just as they received Jesus Christ. We base this conclusion on several reasons. Presumably, if the Paraclete is a person, coming down at a certain definite time to make His abode in the church for guiding, teaching, and sanctifying the body of Christ, there is the same reason for our accepting Him for His special ministry as for accepting the Lord Jesus for His special ministry. To say that in receiving Christ we necessarily received in the same act the gift of the Spirit seems to confound what the Scriptures make distinct.[2] For it is as sinners that we accept Christ for our justification, but it is as sons that we accept the Spirit for our sanctification: "And because ye are sons, God hath sent forth the Spirit of his Son into your hearts crying, Abba, Father" (Gal. 4:6). Thus, when Peter preached his first sermon to the multitude after the Spirit had been given, he said, "Repent, and be baptized every one of you in the name of Jesus Christ for the remission of sins, and ye shall receive the gift of the Holy Ghost" (Acts 2:38).

This passage shows that logically and chronologically the gift of the Spirit is subsequent to repentance. Whether it follows as a necessary and inseparable consequence, as it might seem, we shall consider later. Suffice that this

---

[1] Rev. E. Boys, *Filled with the Spirit*, p. 87.

[2] It is assumed by some that because those who walked with Christ of old received the baptism of the Holy Ghost and fire at Pentecost, more than eighteen hundred years ago, therefore all believers now have received the same. As well might the apostles, when first called, have concluded that because at his baptism the Spirit like a dove rested upon Christ, therefore they had equally received the same blessing. Surely the Spirit has been given and the work in Christ wrought for all; but to enter into possession, to be enlightened and made partakers of the Holy Ghost, there must be a personal application to the Lord, etc. (Andrew Jukes, *The New Man.*)

point is clear, so clear that one of the most conservative as well as ablest writers on this subject, in commenting on this text in Acts, says, "Therefore it is evident that the reception of the Holy Ghost, as here spoken of, has nothing whatever to do with bringing men to believe and repent. It is a subsequent operation; it is an additional and separate blessing; it is a privilege founded on faith already actively working in the heart. . . . I do not mean to deny that the gift of the Holy Ghost may be practically on the same occasion, but never in the same moment. The reason is quite simple too. The gift of the Holy Ghost *is grounded on the fact that we are sons by faith in Christ, believers resting on redemption in Him.* Plainly, therefore, it appears that the Spirit of God has already regenerated us."[3]

As we examine Scripture on this point, we see that we are required to appropriate the Spirit as sons in the same way that we appropriated Christ as sinners. "As many as received him, even to them that believe on his name," is the condition to becoming sons, as we have already seen, receiving and believing being used as equivalent terms. In a type of foretaste of Pentecost, the risen Christ, standing in the midst of His disciples, "breathed on them and saith unto them, Receive ye the Holy Ghost." The verb is not passive, as our English version might lead us to suppose, but has an active meaning, just as in the familiar passage in Revelation: "Whosoever will, let him *take* the water of life freely." Twice in the Epistle to the Galatians the possession of the Holy Spirit is put on the same grounds of active appropriation through faith: "Received ye the Spirit by the works of the law or by the hearing of faith?" (3:2). "That we might receive the promise of the Spirit through faith" (3:14). These texts seem to imply that just as there is a "faith toward our Lord Jesus Christ" for salvation, there is a faith toward the Holy Ghost for power and consecration.

---

[3]William Kelly, *Lectures on the New Testament Doctrine of the Holy Spirit,* p. 161.

If we turn from New Testament teaching to New Testament example, we are strongly confirmed in this impression. We begin with that striking incident in Acts 19. Paul, having found certain disciples at Ephesus, said to them, "Have ye received the Holy Ghost since ye believed? And they said unto him, We have not so much as heard whether there be any Holy Ghost." From this passage it seems decisive that one may be a disciple without having entered into possession of the Spirit as God's gift to believers. Some admit this, and yet deny any possible application of the incident to our own times. They allege that it is the miraculous gifts of the Spirit which are here under consideration—"when Paul had laid his hands upon them, the Holy Ghost came upon them; and they spake with tongues and prophesied." All that need be said upon this point is simply that these Ephesian disciples by the reception of the Spirit came into the same condition with the upper-room disciples who received him some twenty years before, and of whom it is written that "they were all filled with the Holy Ghost, and began to speak with other tongues, as the Spirit gave them utterance" (Acts 2:4). In other words, these Ephesian disciples on receiving the Holy Spirit exhibited the traits of the Spirit common to the other disciples of the apostolic age.

Whether those traits—speaking of tongues and the working of miracles—were intended to be perpetual or not is not within the sphere of our study. But that the presence of the personal Holy Spirit in the church was intended to be perpetual there can be no question. And whatever relationships believers held to that Spirit in the beginning, we have a right to claim today. We must withhold our consent from the inconsistent exegesis which would make the water baptism of the apostolic times still rigidly binding, but would relegate the baptism in the Spirit to a bygone dispensation. We hold, indeed, that Pentecost was once for all, but equally that the appropriation of the Spirit by believers is always for all, and that the shutting up of certain great blessings of the Holy Spirit within that ideal realm called "the apostolic age," however convenient it may be as an escape from imagined difficulties, may be the means of robbing believers of some of their most precious covenant rights.[4]

Let us transfer this incident of the Ephesian Christians to our own times. We need not bring forward an imaginary case, for this same condition is still constantly encountered. Not only individual Christians, but whole communities of believers are found who have been so poorly instructed that they have never known that there is a Holy Spirit, except as an influence, an impersonal something to be vaguely recognized. Of the Holy Spirit as a divine person, dwelling in the church, to be honored and invoked and obeyed and implicitly trusted, they know nothing. Is it conceivable that there could be any deep spiritual life or any real sanctified energy for service in a community like this? And what should be done when discovering a church or an individual Christian in such a condition? Let us turn to another passage of the Acts for an answer: "Now when the apostles which were at Jerusalem heard that Samaria had received the word of God, they sent unto them Peter and John: who, when they were come down, prayed for them, that they might receive the Holy Ghost; for as yet he was fallen upon none of them: only they were baptized in the name of the Lord Jesus. Then laid they their hands on them, and they received the Holy Ghost" (Acts 8:14–17).

Here were believers who had been baptized in water. But this was not enough. The baptism in the Spirit, already bestowed at Pentecost, must be appropriated. Hear the prayer of the apostles: "that they might receive the Holy Ghost." Such prayer we deem eminently proper for

---

[4]It is a great mistake into which some have fallen, to suppose that the results of Pentecost were chiefly miraculous and temporary. The effect of such a view is to keep spiritual influences out of sight; and it will be well ever to hold fast the assurance that a wide, deep, and perpetual spiritual blessing in the church is that which above all things else was secured by the descent of the Spirit after Christ was glorified. (Dr. J. Elder Cumming, *Through the Eternal Spirit*.)

those who today may be ignorant of the Comforter. And yet such prayer should be followed by an act of believing acceptance on the part of the willing disciple: "O Holy Spirit, I yield to you now in humble surrender. I receive you as my Teacher, my Comforter, my Sanctifier, and my Guide." Testimonies abound of new lives resulting from such an act of consecration as this, lives full of peace and power and victory among those who before had received the forgiveness of sins but not the enduement of power.

The primary reason for the enduement of the Spirit concerns our qualification for the highest and most effective service in the church of Christ. Other effects will certainly attend the blessing, but these results will be conducive to the greatest and supreme end, our consecrated usefulness.

Let us observe that Christ, our example in this as in all things, did not enter upon His ministry until He had received the Holy Spirit. Not only so, but we see that all His service from His baptism to His ascension was wrought in the Spirit. Ask concerning His miracles, and we hear Him saying, "I cast out devils by the Spirit of God" (Matt. 12:28). Ask concerning His redemptive death, and we read "who through the eternal Spirit offered himself without spot to God" (Heb. 9:14). Ask concerning the giving of the great commission, and we read that He was received up "after that he through the Holy Ghost had given commandments unto the apostles" (Acts 1:2). Thus, though He was the Son of God, He always acted in supreme reliance upon Him who has been called the "Executive of the Godhead."

Plainly we see how Christ was our pattern in His relation to the Holy Spirit. He had been begotten of the Holy Spirit in the womb of the virgin, and had lived that holy and obedient life which this divine nativity would imply. But when He desired to enter His public ministry, He waited for the Spirit to come *upon* Him, as He had before been *in* Him. For this anointing we find Him praying: "Jesus also being baptized, and praying, the heaven was opened, and the Holy Ghost descended in a bodily shape like a dove upon him" (Luke 3:22). Had He any "promise of the Father" to plead, as He now asked the anointing of the Spirit, if as we may believe this was the subject of His prayer? Yes. It had been written in the prophets concerning the rod out of the stem of Jesse: "And the spirit of the Lord shall rest upon him, the spirit of wisdom and understanding, the spirit of counsel and might, the spirit of knowledge and of the fear of the Lord" (Isa. 11:2). "The promise of the sevenfold Spirit," the Jewish commentators call it. Certainly it was literally fulfilled upon the Son of God at the Jordan when God gave Him the Spirit without measure. For He who was now baptized was in turn to be baptizer. "Upon whom thou shalt see the Spirit descending, and remaining on him, the same is he which baptizeth with the Holy Ghost" (John 1:33). "I indeed baptize you with water unto repentance: but he that cometh after me is mightier that I. . . . he shall baptize you with the Holy Ghost, and with fire" (Matt. 3:11). And now being at the right hand exalted and having "the seven spirits of God" (Rev. 3:1), the fullness of the Holy Spirit, He will shed forth His power upon those who pray for it, even as the Father shed it forth upon himself.

Let us observe now the symbols and descriptions of the enduement of the Spirit which are applied equally to Christ and to the disciples of Christ.

The Sealing of the Spirit

Jesus said to the multitude that sought Him for the loaves and fishes, "Labor not for the meat which perisheth, but for that meat which endureth unto everlasting life, which the Son of man shall give unto you, *for him hath God the Father sealed*" (John 6:27). This sealing must evidently refer back to His reception of the Spirit at the Jordan. One of the most instructive writers on Hebrew worship and ritual tells us that it was the custom for the priest to whom the service pertained to select a lamb from the flock and inspect it with the most minute scrutiny in order to discover if it was without physical defect, and then seal it with the temple seal, thus certifying that it was fit for sacrifice and for food. Behold the Lamb of God presenting himself for inspection at the Jordan! Under the Father's omniscient scrutiny, He is found to be "a lamb without blemish and without spot." From open heaven God gives witness to the fact in the words, "This is my beloved Son in whom I am well pleased"; and then He puts the Holy Spirit upon Him, the testimony to His sonship, the seal of His separation unto sacrifice and service.

The disciple is as his Lord in this experience: "In whom also after that ye believed, ye were sealed with that Holy Spirit of promise" (Eph. 1:13). As always in the statements of Scripture, this transaction is represented as subsequent to faith. It is not conversion, but something done upon a converted soul, a kind of crown of consecration put upon his faith. Indeed, the two events stand in marked contrast. In conversion the believer receives the testimony of God and sets "his seal that God is true" (John 3:33). In consecration God sets His seal upon the believer that He is true. The last is God's "Amen" to the Christian, verifying the Christian's "Amen" to God. "Now he which establisheth us with you in Christ, and hath anointed us, is God; who hath also sealed us, and given the earnest of the Spirit in our hearts" (2 Cor. 1:21, 22).

If we ask to what we are committed and separated by this divine transaction, we may learn by studying a mysterious passage in one of the pastoral epistles. In spite of the defection and unbelief of some, the Apostle says, "Nevertheless the foundation of God standeth sure, having this seal." Then he gives us the two inscriptions on the seal: "The Lord knoweth them that are his" and "Let everyone that nameth the name of Christ depart from iniquity" (2 Tim. 2:19)—*ownership and holiness*. When we receive the gift of the Holy Spirit, it is that we may count ourselves henceforth and altogether Christ's. If we hold back from this commitment, how can we expect the fullness of the Spirit? God cannot put His signature upon what is not

His. If under the sway of a worldly spirit we withhold ourselves from God and insist on self-ownership, we should not think it strange if God withholds himself from us and denies us the seal of divine ownership. God is very jealous of His divine signet. He graciously bestows it upon those who are ready to devote themselves utterly and irrevocably to His service, but He strenuously withholds it from those who, while professing His name, are yet "serving diverse lusts and pleasures." There is a passage in the Gospel of John containing a telling antithesis: "Many trusted in his name, beholding the signs which he did; but Jesus did not trust himself to them" (John 2:23, 24). Here is the great essential to our having the seal of the Spirit. Can the Lord trust us? No; the question is more serious. Can He trust himself to us? Can He commit His signet ring, the Holy Spirit, to our use for signing our prayers and for certifying ourselves, and not compromise His honor?

The other inscription on the seal is: "Let every one that nameth the name of Christ depart from iniquity."[5] The possession of the Spirit commits us irrevocably to separation from sin. For what is holiness but an emanation of the Spirit of holiness who dwells within us? A sanctified life is therefore the print or impression of His seal: "He can never own us without His mark, the stamp of holiness. The devil's stamp is none of God's badge. Our spiritual extraction from Him is but pretended unless we do things worthy of so illustrious birth and becoming the honor of so great a Father." The great office of the Spirit in the present economy is to communicate Christ to His church, His body. And what is so truly essential of Christ as holiness? "In him is no sin; whosoever abideth in him sinneth not" (1 John 3:5, 6). The body can be sinless only by uninterrupted communion with the Head; the Head will not maintain communion with the body except it be holy.

The idea of ownership, just considered, comes out still

---

[5] It will be observed that the inscription on the seal is substantially the same as that upon the forehead of the high priest, "Holiness to the Lord" (Ex. 39:30).

further in the words of the Apostle: "And grieve not the Holy Spirit of God, whereby ye are sealed unto the day of redemption" (Eph. 4:30). The day of redemption is at the advent of our Lord in glory, when He shall raise the dead and translate the living. Now His own are in the world, but the world does not know them. But He has put His mark and secret sign upon them, by which He shall recognize them at His coming. In that great quickening at the Redeemer's advent, the Holy Spirit will be the seal by which the saints will be recognized and the power through which they will be drawn up to God. "If the Spirit of him that raised up Jesus from the dead dwell in you" (Rom. 8:11) is the great condition of final quickening. As a magnet attracts particles of iron and attaches them to itself by first imparting its own magnetism to them, so Christ, having given His Spirit to His own, will draw them to himself through the Spirit. We are not questioning now that all who have eternal life dwelling in them will share in the redemption of the body. We are simply entering into the Apostle's exhortation against grieving the Spirit. We must guard against marring the seal by which we were stamped, lest we deface or obscure the signature by which we are to be recognized in the day of redemption.[6]

The sealing is not an impersonal mark but is the Spirit himself, received by faith and resting upon the believer with all the results in assurance, in joy, and in empowering for service that must follow His unhindered sway in

---

[6]The allusion to the seal as a pledge of purchase would be peculiarly intelligible to the Ephesians, for Ephesus was a maritime city, and an extensive trade in timber was carried on there by the shipmasters of the neighboring ports. The method of purchase was this: The merchant, after selecting his timber, stamped it with his own signet, which was an acknowledged sign of ownership. He often did not carry off his possession at the time; it was left in the harbor with other floats of timber; but it was chosen, bought, and stamped; and in due time the merchant sent a trusty agent with the signet, who finding that timber which bore a corresponding impress, claimed and brought it away for the master's use. Thus the Holy Spirit impresses on the soul now the image of Jesus Christ; and this is the sure pledge of the everlasting inheritance. (E. H. Bickersteth, *The Spirit of Life*, p. 176.)

the soul. Dr. John Owen, who has written more intelligently and more exhaustively on this subject than any with whom I am acquainted, thus sums up the subject: "If we can learn aright how Christ was sealed, we shall learn how we are sealed. The sealing of Christ by the Father is the communication of the Holy Spirit in fullness to him, authorizing him unto and acting his divine power in all the acts and duties of his office, so as to evidence the presence of God with him and approbation of him. God's sealing of believers then is his gracious communication of the Holy Spirit unto them so to act his divine power in them as to enable them unto all the duties of their holy calling, evidencing them to be accepted with him both for themselves and others, and asserting their preservation unto eternal life."[7]

The Filling of the Spirit

Immediately upon Christ's baptism we read: "And Jesus being full of the Holy Ghost returned from the Jordan, and was led by the Spirit into the wilderness" (Luke 4:1). The same record is made concerning the upper-room disciples immediately after the descent of the Spirit: "And they were all filled with the Holy Ghost" (Acts 2:4). What is spoken here seems nothing different from what in other Scriptures is called the reception of the Spirit," an act seemingly distinct from the sealing of the Spirit. It is a transaction that may be repeated, and will be if we are living in the Spirit. But it is clearly an experience belonging to one who has already been converted. This is clearly evidenced in the life of Paul. If the reception of the Spirit is associated always and inseparably with conversion, one will reasonably ask why a conversion so marked and so radical as that of the Apostle Paul need be followed by such an experience as that named in Acts 9:17: "And Ananias went his way and entered into the house; and put-

---

[7]John Owen, D.D., *Discourse Concerning the Spirit*, pp. 406, 407.

ting his hands on him said, Brother Saul, the Lord, even Jesus, that appeared unto thee in the way as thou camest, hath sent me, that thou mightest receive thy sight, and be filled with the Holy Ghost." Here we find a divine something distinct from conversion and subsequent to it, which we have called the reception of the Spirit. "The enduement of power" we may well name it, for observe how constantly throughout the book of Acts mighty works and mighty utterances are connected with this qualification. "Then Peter, *filled with the Holy Ghost*, said unto them" (Acts 4:8), is the preface to one of the Apostle's most powerful sermons. "And they were *all filled with the Holy Ghost*, and they spake the word of God with boldness" (Acts 4:31), is a similar record. And they chose Stephen, a man *full* of faith and *of the Holy Ghost*, the narrative runs, regarding the choice of deacons in Acts 6:5. "And he, being *full of the Holy Ghost*," is the keynote to his great martyr sermon (Acts 7:55). This infilling of the Spirit marks a decisive and most important crisis in the Christian life, judging from Paul's conversion and others to whom we have just referred.

But we do not maintain that this is an experience once for all, as the sealing seems to be. As the words "regeneration" and "renewal" used in Scripture mark respectively the impartation of the divine life as a continuing possession and its increase by repeated communications, so in our sealing there is a one-time reception of the Spirit that may be followed by repeated fillings. It is reasonable to draw this conclusion because our capacity is ever increasing and our need constantly recurring. Godet captures this feeling: "Man is a vessel destined to receive God, a vessel which must be enlarged in proportion as it is filled and filled in proportion as it is enlarged."

And yet I confess a degree of uncertainty about the use of terms, whether the two now under consideration are identical. We may well pause, therefore, and lift a prayer that since "we have received not the spirit of the world but the Spirit which is of God, that we might know the things which are freely given to us of God," this blessed Revelator and Interpreter may not only reveal to us our privilege and inheritance in the Holy Spirit, but teach us to name and distinguish the terms by which it is conveyed.

While the fact of which I speak seems undoubted, the exposition of it is far from easy. Therefore we attach great value to a consensus of opinion on this subject from those who have thought most carefully and searched most prayerfully concerning it. For this reason I have included in this chapter several quotations, believing that the Holy Spirit is most likely to interpret himself through those who most honor Him in seeking His guidance and illumination.

In a recent work on this subject in which careful scholarship and spiritual insight seem well united, the author states his conclusions: "It seems to me beyond question, as a matter of experience both of Christians in the present day and of the early church, as recorded by inspiration, that in addition to the gift of the Spirit received at conversion, there is another blessing received by the apostles at Pentecost—a blessing to be asked for and expected by Christians still, and to be described in language similar to that employed in the book of the Acts. Whatever that blessing may be, it is in immediate connection with the Holy Ghost; and one of the terms by which we may designate it is 'to be filled with the Spirit.' As with the early Christians so with us now, the filling comes when there is special need for it. . . . And there is an occasion when that blessing comes to a man for the first time. That first time is a spiritual crisis from which his future spiritual life must be dated. There may be a question as to what it is to be called, or at least by what name in Scripture we are authorized to call it. . . . Whether consciously or not, it is to the fact of the Holy Spirit's coming in new power to the soul that all new life is due; and the more that this is consciously understood the more is the Holy Ghost in his due place in our hearts. It is only when he is consciously accepted in all his power that we can be said to be either 'baptized' or 'filled' with the Holy Ghost. I should like to add that it is possible to maintain that God from the first offered to his own people a higher position in this matter than they have generally been able to occupy, in that the fullness of the Spirit was and is offered to each soul at conversion; and that it is only from want of faith that subsequent outpourings of the Holy Ghost become needful."[8]

That the filling of the Spirit belongs to us as a covenant privilege seems clear from the exhortation in the Epistle to the Ephesians, which is confessedly of universal application: "Be not drunken with wine, wherein is excess; but be filled with the Spirit" (Eph. 5:18). The passive verb employed here is suggestive. The surrendered will, the yielded body, the emptied heart— these are the great requisites to His incoming. And when He has come and filled the believer, the result is a passive activity, like one worked within and controlled rather than one directing his own efforts. Under the influence of strong drink there is an outpouring of all that its evil inspires—frivolity, profanity, and riotous conduct. "Be God-intoxicated men," the Apostle would seem to say; "let the Spirit of God so control you that you shall pour yourself out in psalms and hymns and spiritual songs." If such divine enthusiasm has its perils, I believe they are less to be dreaded than that "moderatism" which makes the servants of God satisfied with the letter of Scripture if only that letter be skillfully and scientifically handled rather than giving the supreme place to the Spirit as the inspirer and director of all Christian service.

The Anointing of the Spirit

After the baptism and temptation, we find our Lord reading at the Nazareth synagogue, appropriating to himself the words of the prophet: "The Spirit of the Lord is upon me, because he hath anointed me to preach the gospel to the poor" (Luke 4:18). Twice in the Acts there is a reference to this important event in similar terms: "Thy holy child Jesus, whom thou hast anointed" (Acts 4:27).

---

[8]James Elder Cumming, D.D., *Through the Eternal Spirit*, pp. 146, 147.

"How God anointed Jesus of Nazareth with the Holy Ghost and with power" (Acts 10:38). And as with the Lord so with His disciples: "Now he which establisheth us with you in Christ, and hath anointed us, is God" (2 Cor. 1:21).

A student of Scripture need not be told how closely the ceremony of anointing was related to offices and ministries of the servants of Jehovah under the old covenant. The priest was anointed that he might be holy to the Lord (Lev. 8:12). The king was anointed that the Spirit of the Lord might rest on him in power (1 Sam. 16:15). The prophet was anointed that he might be the mouthpiece of God to the people (1 Kings 19:16). No servant of Jehovah was considered qualified for his ministry without this holy, sanctifying touch on him. Even in the cleansing of the leper this ceremony was not lacking. The priest was required to dip his right finger into the oil that was in his left hand and to put it upon the tip of the right ear, upon the thumb of the right hand, upon the great toe of the right foot of him that was to be cleansed, the oil *"upon the blood of the trespass offering"* (Lev. 14:17). Thus with divine accuracy even the types foretold the two-fold provision for the Christian life, cleansing by the blood and hallowing by the oil—justification in Christ, sanctification in the Spirit.

This anointing is obviously the Holy Spirit himself. As before He was the seal confirming us, so now He is the oil sanctifying us—the same gift described by different symbols. And as it was Aaron who had been the first anointed who was then qualified to anoint others, so with our great High Priest. It is He within the veil who gives the Spirit to His own, that He may qualify them to be "a chosen generation, a royal priesthood, a holy nation, a peculiar people" (1 Pet. 2:9). "But ye have an unction [anointing] from the Holy One, and ye know all things" (1 John 2:20). Christ in the New Testament is constantly called "the Holy One." And because the Spirit was sent to communicate Him to the people, they are made partakers of His knowledge as well as of His holiness. If it should be said that this unction John speaks of is miraculous, the divine il-

lumination of evangelists and prophets who were commissioned to be the vehicles of inspired Scripture, we must
call attention to other passages which connect the knowledge of God with the Holy Spirit. "For what man knoweth
the things of a man, save the spirit of a man which is in
him? even so the things of God knoweth no man, but the
Spirit of God" (1 Cor. 2:11). The horse and rider may see
the same magnificent statue in the park; the one may be
delighted with it as a work of human genius, but upon the
dull eye of the other it makes no impression, because it
takes a human mind to appreciate the work of the human
mind. Likewise only the Spirit of God can know and make
known the thoughts and teachings and revelations of God.
This seems to be the meaning of John in his discourse
concerning the divine unction: "But the anointing which
ye have received of him abideth in you, and ye need not
that any man teach you; but as the same anointing teacheth you of all things" (1 John 2:17).

The enduement of the Spirit distinctly manifests itself
in the tuned discernment of revealed truth that it imparts.
In service, the contrast between working in the power of
the Spirit and in the energy of the flesh is easily discern-
ible. Even more clearly in knowledge and teaching is the
contrast between the instruction of learning and the in-
tuition of the Spirit. While we should not undervalue the
former, it is striking to note how the Bible puts the weight-
ier emphasis on the latter. When, for example, one at-
tempts with the utmost learning to convince an unbeliever
of the deity of Christ and fails, the word of Scripture to
him is: "No man can say that Jesus is the Lord, but by the
Holy Ghost" (1 Cor. 12:3).

The Spirit of Jesus alone can reveal to men the lordship
of Jesus, and this key of knowledge the Holy Spirit will
never put into the hand of any man learned or unlearned.
It is written that Christ is the "raying forth" of the Father's glory, and "the express image of his person" (Heb.
1:3). This beautiful figure reminds us that as we can see
the sun only in the rays of the sun, so we can know God

only in Jesus Christ, the manifestation of God. It is likewise this way between the second and third Persons of the Trinity. Christ is the image of the invisible God; the Holy Spirit is the invisible image of Christ. As Jesus manifested the Father outwardly, the Spirit manifests Jesus inwardly, forming Him within us as the hidden man of the heart, an interior impression on man's spirit which no intellectual instruction, however diligent, can effect.

In his profound discourse concerning "unction" and accompanying illumination, John was only expounding by the Spirit what Jesus had said before His departure: "Howbeit when he, the Spirit of truth, is come, he will guide you into all truth. . . . He shall glorify me; for he shall receive of mine and shall show it unto you" (John 16:13, 14). "The Spirit of truth"—how much instruction is conveyed by this term! As He is called "the Spirit of Christ," revealing Christ in His suffering and glory, so He is called "the Spirit of truth," manifesting the truth in all its depths and heights. As impossible as it is to know the person of Christ without the Spirit of Christ who reveals Him, so impossible it is to know the truth as it is in Jesus without the Spirit of truth who is appointed to convey it. "The Spirit of truth, whom the world cannot receive" (John 14:17)—we must come to Christ before the Spirit can come to us. "The Spirit of truth, which proceedeth from the Father" (John 15:26)—He can teach us only in intelligent sonship to cry, "Abba, Father." "The Spirit of truth . . . shall guide you into all truth" (John 16:13). Divine knowledge is all and altogether in His power to communicate, and without His illumination it must be hidden from our understanding.

Thus we have had the enduement of the Spirit presented to us under three aspects: sealing, filling, and anointing. Each term, so far as we can understand, signify the same thing—the gift of the Holy Ghost appropriated through faith. Each is connected with some special Divine endowment—the seal with assurance and consecration; the filling with power; and the anointing with knowledge. All these gifts are wrapped up in the one gift of the Spirit, without whom we are excluded from possessing them.

While we conclude that it is a Christian's privilege and duty to claim a distinct anointing of the Spirit to qualify him for his work, we would be careful not to prescribe any stereotyped exercises through which one must necessarily pass in order to possess it. It is easy to cite cases of decisive, vivid, and clearly marked experiences of the Spirit's enduement, as in the lives of Dr. Finney, James Brainard Taylor, and many others. Instead of discrediting these experiences—definite in occurrence yet distinct in accompanying credentials—we would ask the reader to study them and observe the remarkable effects that followed in the ministry of those who enjoyed them. The lives of many of the co-laborers with Wesley and Whitefield strikingly confirm the doctrine we are defending. Years of barren ministry in which the gospel was preached with orthodox correctness and literary excellence were followed by evangelistic pastorates of the most fervent type once the Holy Spirit had been recognized and appropriated. We need guard this great subject from too minute theological definitions on the one hand and too exacting demands for striking spiritual exercises on the other, lest we put upon believers burdens greater than they can bear. Nevertheless, we cannot emphasize too strongly the divine crisis in the soul which a full reception of the Holy Spirit may bring. "My little children, of whom I travail in birth again until Christ be formed in you" (Gal. 4:19), writes the Apostle to those who had already believed on the Son of God. Whatever he may have meant in this fervent saying, we do not doubt that the deepest yearning of the Spirit is for the informing of Christ in the heart so that the outward conformity to Christ, the goal of Christian nurture, would be accomplished. If we conceive of the Christian life as only a gradual growth in grace, is there not danger that we come to regard this growth as both invisible and inevitable, and so take little responsibility for its accomplishment? Let the believer receive the Holy Spirit by a definite act of faith for his consecration, as he received Christ by faith for his justification, and he may be sure that he is in a safe and scriptural way of acting. We know of no plainer form of stating the matter than to speak of it as a simple acceptance by faith.

It is a fact that Christ has made atonement for sin. In conversion faith appropriates this fact for justification. It is also a fact that the Holy Spirit has been given and that in consecration faith appropriates this fact for our sanctification. One who writes on this subject with a scholarship evidently illuminated by a deep spiritual instruction says: "If a reference to personal experience may be permitted, I may indeed here 'set my seal.' Never shall I forget the gain to conscious faith and peace which came to my own soul, not long after a first decisive and appropriating view of the crucified Lord as the sinner's sacrifice of peace, from a more intelligent and conscious hold upon the living and most gracious personality of the Spirit through whose mercy the soul had got that blessed view. It was a new development of insight into the love of God. It was a new contact as it were with the inner and eternal movements of redeeming goodness and power, a new discovery in divine resources."[9]

Well is our doctrine described in these words: "*A contact with the inner movements of Divine power.*" The energy of the Spirit appropriated is like the uplifted finger of the electric car that touches the current moving just above it in the wire. The car is borne irresistibly on by it—thus does the power which is eternally for us become a power within us. The law of Sinai, with its tables of stone, is replaced by "the law of the Spirit of life" in the fleshly tables of the heart, the outward commandment is exchanged for an inward rule, and hard duty by holy delight, that henceforth the Christian life may be "all in Christ, by the Holy Spirit, for the glory of God."

---

[9] Principal H.C.G. Moule, *Veni Creator Spiritus*, p. 13.

"In his intimate union with his Son, the Holy Spirit is the unique organ by which God wills to communicate to man his own life, the supernatural life, the divine life—that is to say, his holiness, his power, his love, his felicity. To this end the Son works outwardly, the Holy Spirit inwardly."
—Pastor G. F. Tophel

6

The Communion of the Spirit

The familiar benediction of the "communion of the Holy Ghost" contains a deeper meaning than has generally been recognized. The word "communion"—*koinonia*—signifies "the having in common." It is used of the fellowship of believers one with another and also of their mutual fellowship with God. The Holy Spirit dwelling in us is the agent through whom this community of life and love is effected and maintained. "And truly our fellowship," says John, "is with the Father and with his Son Jesus Christ" (1 John 1:3). But having this fellowship with the first two Persons of the Godhead is only possible through the communion of the Holy Spirit, the third Person. In His promise of the Comforter, Jesus said: "He shall take of mine and show it unto you." As the Son while on earth communicated to men the spiritual riches of the invisible Father, so the Spirit now communicates to us the hidden things of the invisible Son; and if we were required to describe in a word the present ministry of the Holy Spirit, we should say that it is to make real *in* us that which is already true *for* us in our glorified Lord. All light and life and warmth are stored up for us in the sun; but these can reach us only through the atmosphere standing between us and the sun as the medium of communication. Even so in Christ are "hidden all the treasures of wisdom and knowledge," and by the Holy Spirit these are brought to us. It is our intention in this chapter to consider our treasures in Christ, and to consider the Spirit in His various offices of communication.

The Spirit of Life: Our Regeneration

Not until our Lord took His place at God's right hand did He assume His full prerogative as life-giver to us. Jesus took on our nature that He might in himself crucify our Adam-life and put it away. But when He rose from the dead and sat down on His Father's throne, He became the life-giver to all His mystical body, the church. To talk of being saved by the earthly life of Jesus is to know Christ only "after the flesh." True, the Apostle says that "being reconciled" by Christ's death, "much more being reconciled we shall be saved by his life." But he here refers plainly to Christ's glorified life. And Jesus, looking forward to the time when He would rise from the dead, says, "Because I live, ye shall live also." Christ on the throne is really the heart of the church, and every regeneration is a pulse beat of that heart in souls begotten from above through the Holy Spirit.

The new birth therefore is not a change of nature as it is sometimes defined; it is rather the communication of the divine nature, and the Holy Spirit is now the Mediator through whom this life is transmitted. If we take our Lord's words to Nicodemus, "Except a man be born again, he cannot see the kingdom of God," and press the "again"— *anothen*—back to its deepest significance, it becomes very instructive. "Born *from above*," say some. And this wording is very true. Regeneration is not our natural life carried up to its highest point of attainment, but the divine life brought down to its lowest point of condescension, even to the heart of fallen man. John, in speaking of Jesus as the life-giver, calls him "*he that cometh from above*" (3:31); and Jesus, in speaking to the degenerate sons of Abraham, says, "Ye are *from beneath*; I am *from above*" (John 8:23).

It has been the constant dream and delusion of men that they could rise to heaven by the development and improvement of their natural life. Jesus by one stroke of revelation destroys this hope, telling His hearers that unless they have been supernaturally born of God, as truly as they have been born of a father on earth, they will not see the kingdom of God.

Others make these words of our Lord signify "born *from the beginning*." This implies a return to the original source and fountain of being. To find this it is not enough that we go back to the creation-beginning revealed in Genesis; we must return to the precreation-beginning revealed in John. In the opening of Genesis we find Adam, created holy, now fallen through temptation, his face turned from God and leading the whole human race after him into sin and death. In the opening of the Gospel of John we find the Son of God in holy fellowship with the Father. "In the beginning was the Word, and the Word was with [toward] God, *pros ton theon*"—not merely proceeding from God, but tending toward God by eternal communion. Conversion restores man to this lost attitude: "Ye turned to God, *pros ton theon*, from idols to serve the living and true God" (1 Thess. 1:9). Regeneration restores man to his forfeited life, the unfallen life of the Son of God, the life which has never wavered from the steadfast fellowship with the Father. "I give unto them eternal life," says Jesus. Is eternal life without end? Yes, and it is just as truly without beginning. It is uncreated being in distinction from all-created being, the I-am life of God in contrast to the I-become life of all human souls. By spiritual birth we acquire a divine heredity as truly as by natural birth we acquire a human heredity.

In the condensed antithesis with which our Lord concludes His demand for the new birth, we have both the philosophy and the justification of His doctrine: "That which is born of the flesh is flesh; and that which is born of the Spirit is spirit. Marvel not that I said unto thee, Ye must be born again" (John 3:7). By no process of evolution,

however prolonged, can the natural man be developed into
the spiritual man. These two are from a totally different
stock and origin. The one is from beneath, the other is
from above. There is but one way through which the relation of sonship can be established, and that is by birth.
That God has created all men does not constitute them
His sons in the evangelical sense of that word. The sonship
on which the New Testament dwells so constantly is based
absolutely and solely on the experience of the new birth,
while the doctrine of universal sonship rests either upon
a daring denial of the universal fall of man through sin,
or the assumption of the universal regeneration of man
through the Spirit. In either case the teaching belongs to
"another gospel."

The contrast between the two lives and the way in
which the partnership—the *koinonia*—with the new is effected, is told in that deep saying of Peter: "Whereby are
given unto us exceeding great and precious promises: that
by these ye might be partakers—*koinonoi*—of the divine
nature, having escaped the corruption that is in the world
through lust" (2 Pet. 1:4). Here the two streams of life are
contrasted:

1. The corruption in the world through lust.

2. The divine nature which is in the world through the
incarnation.

Here is the self-life into which we have joined ourselves
with Adam; and over against it the Christ-life into which
we are brought by spiritual birth. From the one we escape,
of the other we partake. The source and results of the one
are briefly summarized: "When lust hath conceived, it
bringeth forth sin: and sin, when it is finished, bringeth
forth death" (James 1:15). The Jordan is a fitting symbol
of our natural life, rising in a lofty elevation and from
pure springs, but plunging steadily down till it pours itself
into that Dead Sea from which there is no outlet. To be
taken out of this stream and to be brought into the life
which flows from the heart of God is man's only hope of
salvation. And the method of effecting this transition is

plainly stated, "through these," the precious and exceeding great promises. In grafting, the old and degenerate stock must first be cut off and then the new inserted. In regeneration we are separated from the flesh and incorporated by the Spirit. The word or promise of God is the medium through which the Holy Spirit is conveyed, the germ cell in which the divine life is enfolded. Thus, the emphasis is put in Scripture upon the appropriation of divine truth. We are told that "of his own will begat he us *with the word of truth*" (James 1:18). "Being born again, not of corruptible seed, but of incorruptible, *by the word of God*, which liveth and abideth" (1 Pet. 1:23).

Very deep and significant, therefore, is the saying of Jesus in respect to the regenerating power of His words in John 6. He contrasts the two natures, the human and the divine, saying, "It is the spirit that quickeneth; the flesh profiteth nothing" (v. 63). And then He adds, "The words that I speak unto you, they are spirit and they are life" (v. 64). As God in creation breathed into man the breath of life and he became a living soul, so the Lord Jesus by the word of His mouth, the breath of life, recreates man and makes him alive unto God.

And not life only, but likeness as well, is thus imparted. Through the fall man had not only lost spiritual life, he had lost the spiritual image of God. The notion is persistent and seems incurable in the human heart, that whatever may have been lost from the original type, education and training can reshape. Here again we refer to the authoritative teaching of Jesus Christ: "A good tree cannot bring forth evil fruit, neither can a corrupt tree bring forth good fruit." The problem is the life source. The only remedy for a corrupt tree is to cut off the old and bring in a new life source and stock. The life of God can alone give birth to the likeness of God; the divine type is wrapped up in the same germ which holds the divine nature. Therefore in regeneration we are said to have "put on the new man, which is renewed in knowledge *after the image of him that created him*" (Col. 3:10), and "which *after God* is created in . . . true holiness" (Eph. 4:24).

In a word, the spiritual image of God is not restamped upon us, but renewed within us. Christ our life was "begotten of the Holy Ghost," and He became the fount and origin of life henceforth for all His church. This communication of the divine life from Christ to the soul through the Holy Spirit is a hidden transaction, but so great in its significant results that one has well called it "the greatest of all miracles." In the origin of our natural life we are made in secret and curiously wrought; much more are we in our spiritual. But the issue has to do with the farthest eternity. "As when the Lord was born, the world still went on its old way, little conscious that one had come who should one day change and rule all things, so when the new man is framed within, the old life for a while goes on much as before; the daily calling, and the earthly cares, and too often old lusts and habits also, still ingross us; a worldly eye sees little new, while yet the life which shall live forever has been quickened within and a new man been formed who shall inherit all."[1]

The Spirit of Holiness: Our Sanctification

"According to the Spirit of holiness," Christ "was declared to be the Son of God with power by the resurrection from the dead" (Rom. 1:4). How striking is the antithesis between our Lord's two natures, as revealed in this passage: Son of David as to the flesh (1:3), Son of God as to the Spirit. And "as he is so are we in this world." We who are regenerate have two lives; the natural life derived from the flesh, the other derived from Christ. Our sanctification consists in the double process of deadening and subduing the old and quickening and developing the new. In other words, what was accomplished in Christ who was "put to death in the flesh but quickened in the spirit" is also accomplished in us through the constant operation of the

---

[1]Andrew Jukes, *The New Man*, p. 53.

Holy Spirit, and thus the cross and the resurrection extend their sway over the entire life of the Christian. Consider these two experiences.

Biblically, mortification is not asceticism. It is not self-inflicted penitence, but a Christ-inflicted crucifixion. Our Lord was done with the cross when on Calvary He cried, "It is finished!" But where He ended, each disciple must begin: "If any man will come after me, let him deny himself, and take up his cross, and follow me. For whosoever will save his life shall lose it, and whosoever will lose his life for my sake shall find it" (Matt. 16:24, 25). These words, so constantly repeated in one form or another by our Lord, make it clear that the death-principle must be realized within us in order that the life-principle may have final and triumphant sway. It is to this truth which every disciple is solemnly committed in his baptism: "Know ye not, that so many of us as were baptized into Jesus Christ were baptized into his death? Therefore we are buried with him by baptism into death: that like as Christ was raised up from the dead by the glory of the Father, even so we also should walk in newness of life" (Rom. 6:3, 4). Baptism is the monogram of the Christian; by it every believer is sealed and certified as a participant in the death and life of Christ. The Holy Spirit has been given to be the Executor of that contract.

In considering the great fact of the believer's death in Christ to sin and the law, we must not confound what the Scriptures clearly distinguish. There are three deaths in which we have part:

1. *Death in sin, our natural condition.* "And you . . . who were dead in trespasses and sins," "And you, being dead in your sins" (Eph. 2:1; Col. 2:13). This is the condition in which we find ourselves as participants in the fall and ruin into which the transgression of our first parents has plunged the race. It is a condition in which we are under moral unconsciousness to the claims of God's holiness and love and under the sentence of eternal punishment from the law which we have broken. In this state of

death in sin Christ found the whole world when He came to be our Savior.

2. *Death for sin, our judicial condition.* "Wherefore, my brethren, ye also are become dead to the law by the body of Christ" (Rom. 7:4). This is the condition into which Christ brought us by His sacrifice upon the cross. He endured the sentence of a violated law on our behalf, and therefore we are counted as having endured it in Him. What He did for us is reckoned as having been done by us: "Because we thus judge, that if one died for all, then were all dead" (2 Cor. 5:14). Being one with Christ through faith, we are identified with Him on the cross: "I am crucified with Christ" (Gal. 2:20). This condition of death for sin having been effected for us by our Savior, we are held legally or judicially free from the penalty of a violated law, if by our personal faith we will consent to the transaction.

3. *Death to sin, our sanctified condition.* "Reckon ye also yourselves to be dead indeed unto sin, but alive unto God through Jesus Christ our Lord" (Rom. 6:11). This is the condition of making real in us what is already true for us in Christ, of rendering practical what is now judicial— in other words, of being dead to the power of sin in ourselves, as we are already dead to the penalty of sin through Jesus Christ. As it is written: "For ye are dead," judicially in Christ, "mortify [make dead practically] therefore your members which are upon the earth" (Col. 3:3, 5). It is this condition that the Holy Spirit is constantly effecting in us if we will have it so. "If ye through the Spirit do mortify the deeds of the body, ye shall live" (Rom. 8:13). This is not self-deadening, as the Revised Version seems to suggest by its decapitalization of the word "spirit." Self is not powerful enough to conquer self, the human spirit to get the victory over the human flesh. "Old Adam is too strong for young Melancthon," said the Reformer. It is the Spirit of God overcoming our fleshly nature by His indwelling life on whom we solely depend. Our principal care therefore must be to "walk in the Spirit" and "be filled with the Spirit," and all the rest will come spontaneously and inevitably.

One cannot fail to see that asceticism is an absolute inversion of the divine order. No degree of self-mortification can ever bring us to sanctification. We are to "put off concerning the former conversation the old man." But how? By putting "on the new man, which after God is created in righteousness and true holiness" (Eph. 4:22, 24). "For the law of the Spirit of life in Christ Jesus hath made me free from the law of sin and death" (Rom. 8:2), writes Paul. No amount of self-mortification that is directed at changing the deep-rooted habits and evil tendencies of the old man—its selfishness, its pride, its lust, and its vanity—will effect real change. The only way to change is to bring in the Spirit, to drink in His divine presence, to breathe, as a holy atmosphere, His supernatural life. The indwelling of the Spirit alone can effect the exclusion of sin. This will appear if we consider what has been called "the expulsive power of a new affection." "Love not the world, neither the things that are in the world," says the Scripture. But all experience proves that "loving not" is only possible through loving, the worldly affection overcome by the heavenly.

And we find this method clearly exhibited in the word. "The love of the Spirit" (Rom. 15:30) is given us for overcoming the world. The divine life is the source of the divine love. Therefore "the love of God is shed abroad in our hearts by the Holy Ghost which is given unto us" (Rom. 5:5). God transforms our loveless hearts by placing His own love within us through the indwelling Spirit. Herein is the highest credential of discipleship: "By this shall all men know that ye are my disciples, if ye have love one to another" (John 13:35). Christ manifested to the world the love of the Father, and we are to manifest the love of Christ—a manifestation, however, which is only possible because of our possessorship of a common life. As one has truly said concerning our Savior's command to love one another: "It is a command which would be utterly idle and futile were it not that He, the ever-loving One, is willing to put His own love within me. The command is really no

more than to be a branch of the true vine. I am to cease
from my own living and loving, and yield myself to the
expression of Christ's love."

And what is true of the love of Christ is true of the
likeness of Christ. How is the likeness acquired? Through
meditation and imitation? So some have taught. Scripture
indicates the real way: "But we all, with open face beholding as in a glass the glory of the Lord, are changed
into the same image from glory to glory, even as by the
Spirit of the Lord" (2 Cor. 3:18). It is only the Spirit of the
Lord dwelling within us that can change us to the image
of the Lord set before us. Who is sufficient by external
imitation of Christ to become conformed to the likeness of
Christ? Imagine yourself sitting down before Raphael's
famous picture of the transfiguration and attempting to
reproduce it. Impossible, you say. But if it were possible
that the spirit of Raphael should enter you and obtain the
mastery of your mind and eye and hand, it would be entirely possible that you should paint this masterpiece; for
it would simply be Raphael reproducing Raphael. And this
in a mystery is what is true of the disciple filled with the
Holy Spirit. Christ, who is "the image of the invisible God,"
is set before him as his divine pattern, and Christ is able
to image forth Christ from the interior life to the outward
example.

Of course likeness to Christ is but another name for
holiness, and when at the resurrection, we awake satisfied
with His likeness (Ps. 17:15), we shall be perfected in holiness. This is simply saying that sanctification is progressive and not, like conversion, instantaneous. And yet
there is a danger of regarding it as *only* a gradual growth.
If a Christian looks upon himself as "a tree planted by the
rivers of water, that bringeth forth his fruit in his season,"
he judges rightly. But to conclude therefore that his growth
will be as irresistible as that of the tree, coming simply
because he has by regeneration been planted in Christ, is
a grave mistake. The disciple is required to be consciously
and intelligently active in his own growth as a tree is not,

"to give diligence to make your calling and election sure" (2 Pet. 1:10). And when we say "active," we do not mean self-active, but that we must surrender ourselves to the divine action by living in the Spirit and praying in the Spirit and walking in the Spirit, all of which are as essential to our development in holiness as the rain and the sunshine are to the growth of the oak. It is possible that through a neglect and grieving of the Spirit a Christian may be in spiritual retrogression rather than in advance. Therefore, in saying that sanctification is progressive, let us beware of concluding that it is inevitable.

Moreover, we must ask about the validity of the doctrine of "instantaneous sanctification," which many devout persons teach and profess to have experienced. If the conception is that of a state of sinless perfection into which the believer has been suddenly lifted, we must consider this doctrine as dangerously untrue. But we do consider it possible that one may experience a great crisis in his spiritual life, in which there is such a total self-surrender to God and such an infilling of the Holy Spirit, that he is freed from the bondage of sinful appetites and habits, and enabled to have constant victory over self instead of suffering constant defeat. In saying this, what more do we affirm than is taught in that verse: "Walk in the Spirit, and ye shall not fulfill the lust of the flesh" (Gal. 5:16).

Divine truth as revealed in Scripture seems often to lie between two extremes. It is emphatically so in regard to this question. What a paradox it is that side by side in the Epistle of John we should have a negative affirmation of the Christian's life: "If we say that we have no sin, we deceive ourselves, and the truth is not in us"; and a positive affirmation: "Whosoever is born of God doth not commit sin; for his seed remaineth in him: and he cannot sin, because he is born of God" (1 John 1:8; 3:9). Now heresy means a dividing or choosing, and almost all the gravest errors have arisen from adopting some extreme statement of Scripture to the rejection of the other extreme. If we regard the doctrine of sinless perfection as heresy, we regard contentment with sinful imperfection as a greater heresy. And we gravely fear that many Christians make the Apostle's words the unconscious justification for a low standard of Christian living. It would almost be better for one to overstate the possibilities of sanctification in his eager grasp after holiness than to understate them in his complacent satisfaction with a traditional unholiness. Certainly it is not an edifying spectacle to see a Christian worldling throwing stones at a Christian perfectionist.

What then would be a true statement of the doctrine which we are considering, one which would embrace both extremes of statement as they appear in the Epistle of John? *Sinful in self, sinless in Christ* is our answer: "In him is no sin; whosoever abideth in him sinneth not" (1 John 3:5, 6). If through the communication of the Holy Spirit the life of Christ is constantly imparted to us, that life will prevail within us. That life is absolutely sinless, as incapable of defilement as the sunbeam which has its fount and origin in the sun. In proportion to the closeness of our abiding in Him will be the completeness of our deliverance from sinning. For those who yield themselves to God in absolute surrender, and who through the upholding power of the Spirit are kept in that condition of surrender, sin will not have dominion over them (Rom. 6:14). The fleshly life has been crucified (Gal. 5:24), there has been present victory in which troublesome sins have ceased from their assaults, and "the peace of God" has ruled in the heart. He may still stumble and fall into a sin, but he quickly comes to the cleansing blood and is renewed in the Spirit. Sin has lost its dominion.

The Spirit of Glory: Our Transfiguration

"The Spirit of glory and of God resteth upon you," writes Peter (1 Pet. 4:14). Let us recall this apostle's habit of dividing the stages of redemption into these two, "the sufferings of Christ and the glory that should follow," in which he seems to conceive of our Lord's mystical body, the church, as passing through and reproducing the twofold experience of its Head, in humiliation and in subsequent exaltation. Even in the time of her humiliation, she has the Spirit of glory abiding on her as the cloud of glory rested on the tabernacle in the wilderness during all the pilgrimage of the children of Israel. And is this not the same as Paul's picture of the suffering creation: "But ourselves also, which have the first-fruits of the spirit, even we ourselves groan within ourselves, waiting for the adoption, to wit, the redemption of our body" (Rom. 8:23). We have not yet reached the consummation of our hope, at the "glorious appearing of the great God and our Savior Jesus Christ" (Titus 2:13); but the Spirit, through whose inworking power this great change is to be accomplished, already dwells in us, giving us by His present quickening the assurance and down payment of our final glory. And so we read in another verse: "But if the Spirit of him that raised up Jesus from the dead dwell in you, he that raised up Christ from the dead shall also quicken your mortal bodies by his Spirit that dwelleth in you" (Rom. 8:11). It is not our dead bodies which are here spoken of as the objects of the Spirit's quickening, but our mortal bodies—bodies liable to death and doomed to death, but not yet having experienced death. Hence the quickening referred to has to do with living saints.

Of course the consummation of this quickening is at the Lord's coming, when those who have died shall be raised and those who are alive shall be transfigured; but because of the Spirit of life dwelling in us, who shall say that the process has not even now begun? To explain: "Behold, I shew you a mystery," says Paul; "we shall not all sleep, but we shall all be changed, in a moment, in the twinkling of an eye, at the last trump" (1 Cor. 15:51, 52). That is, at Christ's coming the dead saints will be raised and the living saints will be translated without seeing death. A change will come to them, so far as we can understand, like that which came to Jesus at His resurrection—the body glorified, all of its mortality eliminated in an instant, and the Holy Spirit so completely transforming and immortalizing it that it shall become perfectly fashioned to the likeness of Christ's glorified body. Now, through the Spirit's indwelling, we have the firstfruits of this transformation in the daily renewing of our inward man, in the helping and healing and strengthening which sometimes comes to our bodies. Sanctification is progressive, waiting to be consummated in the future; glorification is also in some sense progressive, since by the presence of the Spirit we already have the down payment of the glory that is to be. Edward Irving beautifully states: "As sickness in the body is the presentiment of death the forerunner of corruption, and as disease of every kind is mortality begun, so the quickening of our mortal bodies by the inward inspiration of the Spirit is the resurrection forestalled, redemption anticipated, glory begun in our humiliation."

When is sanctification completed? At death is the answer which we find given in some creeds and manuals of theology. As far as we can infer from the Word of God, the date of our sanctification or perfection in holiness is definitely fixed at the appearing of the Lord "a second time without sin unto salvation." Our sanctification, now going on, is glory completed in us. The Spirit of glory now working in us brings forward and already works within us the beginning of the perfect life. Because we have been made "partakers of the Holy Ghost," we have thereby "tasted . . . the powers of the world to come" (Heb. 6:4, 5), that age of complete deliverance from sin and sickness and death. We have only tasted it; we have not drunk fully into the fountain of immortal life. It is at Christ's advent that this blessed consummation is fixed: "To the end he may establish your hearts unblameable in holiness before God, even our Father, *at the coming of our Lord Jesus with all his saints*" (1 Thess. 3:13). Not simply blameless, but faultless, seems to be the condition here foretold, since it is unblameable in the sphere and element of holiness.

And with this agrees another text in the same epistle:

"And the very God of peace sanctify you wholly; and I pray your whole spirit and soul and body be preserved blameless unto the coming of our Lord Jesus Christ" (1 Thess. 5:23). The time appointed for the consummation of this blameless wholeness is at the Savior's advent in glory. And how suggestive is the order maintained in naming the threefold man: "Your spirit, soul, and body." Our sanctification moves from within outward. It begins with the spirit, which is the holy of holies; the Spirit of God acting first on the spirit of man in renewing grace, then upon the soul till at last it reaches the outer court of the body at the resurrection and translation. When the body is glorified, then only will sanctification be consummated, for then only will the whole man—spirit, soul, and body—have come under the Spirit's perfecting power.

We may see the difference between progressive sanctification and perfected sanctification, or glorification, by comparing familiar texts. One already has been quoted in this chapter: "We all with open face beholding as in a glass the glory of the Lord, are changed into the same image from glory to glory, even as by the Spirit of the Lord" (2 Cor. 3:18). Here are degrees of progress "from glory to glory," and it is a progress in the glorified life—gradual conformity to the Lord of glory, through successive stages of glory, effected by the Spirit of glory. The word-painting of the passage inevitably associates itself with the great transfiguration experience of our Lord, when by a kind of rapture He was for a little while taken out of "this present evil age" (Gal. 1:4), and translated into "the age to come," and made to taste of its powers as He appeared in glory (Heb. 6:5). So says the Apostle, "Be not conformed to this world [age]: but be ye transformed by the renewing of your mind" (Rom. 12:2). That is, by his inward transformation, the Holy Spirit is to be daily repeating in us the Lord's glorification, separating us from the present age of sin and death and assimilating us to the age to come. Then is resurrection triumph and perfected restoration to God, when we shall be presented "faultless before the presence of his glory with exceeding joy" (Jude 24).

This is our step-by-step advancement into a predestined inheritance; and it must for the present be step by step. "Of his fulness have all we received," but we can appropriate that fulness only "grace for grace" (John 1:16). Of His righteousness we have all been made partakers, but we only advance in its possession "from faith to faith" (Rom. 1:17). Even in passing through the valley of Baca we can make it a place of springs, going "from strength to strength" as we appear in Zion "before God" (Ps. 84:7). Thus our growth in grace is our glory begun, but the progress is like the artist's slow and patient perfecting of his picture.

Turn now to another statement: "We know that, when he shall appear, we shall be like him; for we shall see him as he is" (1 John 3:2). One thought seems to be taught throughout that the unveiled manifestation of God will bring the full perfection of His saints. Thus Alford says that as the believer "becomes more and more like God, having his seed in him, so the full and perfect accomplishment of this knowledge in the actual fruition of God himself must of necessity bring with it entire likeness to God." "In a moment, in the twinkling of an eye . . . we shall be changed" (1 Cor. 15:52). Then the glorified body and the glorified spirit, long divorced by sin, will be remarried. As long as they are separated, our final perfection in holiness is impossible.

The perfection of the resurrection state is found in this saying: "It is raised a spiritual body" (1 Cor. 15:44). *Now*, how often has the body dominated the spirit, making it do what it does not desire; but *then*, the spirit will dominate the body, making it do its will. The condition in our present state of humiliation, our mortal body, is far from perfect and often hinders us. And not the body alone, but the soul and its functions are far from perfect. Though renewed and capable of service for God, the mind, emotions, and will are vulnerable to attack and often are found to yield to fleshly desires. The whole man must be presented blameless at the coming of the Lord before we can enter upon a state of absolute perfection. Our spirit must not only rule our soul and our body, but both these must be subject to the Holy Spirit of God. Dimly and imperfectly do we thus image the perfection of our "spiritual body." Nevertheless, we are "to press toward the mark for the prize of the high calling of God in Christ" (Phil. 3:14). Like a runner we strive forward toward Christlikeness, despite the limitations. The day will come when the Holy Spirit by His divine inworking, will complete in us the divine likeness and perfect over us the divine dominion. The human body will be in sovereign subjection to the human spirit, and the human spirit to the divine Spirit, and God will be all and in all.

"The Holy Ghost from the day of Pentecost has occupied an entirely new position. The whole administration of the affairs of the Church of Christ has since that day devolved upon him. . . . That day was the installation of the Holy Spirit as the Administrator of the Church in all things, which office he is to exercise according to circumstances at his discretion. It is as vested with such authority that he gives his name to this dispensation. . . . There is but one other great event to which the Scripture directs us to look, and that is the second coming of the Lord. Till then we live in the Pentecostal age and under the rule of the Holy Ghost."

—James Elder Cumming, D.D.

7

The Administration of the Spirit

The Holy Spirit, as sent to fill the place of the ascended Redeemer, has rightly been called "The Vicar of Jesus Christ." To Him the entire administration of the church has been committed until Jesus returns. His management extends to the slightest detail in the ordering of God's house, holding all in subjection to the will of the Head and directing all in harmony with the divine plan. How clearly this comes out in First Corinthians 12—concerning the "diversities of administrations" determined by the one Administrator, the Holy Spirit. "Diversities of gifts, but *the same Spirit*"; "diversities of operations, but *the same God*"; "the word of knowledge by *the same Spirit*"; "faith by *the same Spirit*"; "gifts of healing by *the same Spirit*"; miracles, prophecies, tongues, interpretations, "but all these worketh the one and the selfsame Spirit, dividing to every man severally as he will." Whether the authority of the Holy Spirit is recognized or ignored determines whether the church shall be an anarchy or a unity, a synagogue of lawless ones or the temple of the living God.

Here one finds the clue to the great apostasy whose dark eclipse now covers so much of Christendom—the rule and authority of the Holy Spirit ignored in the church, the servants of the house assuming mastery and encroaching more and more on the prerogatives of the Head, till often one man is set up as the administrator of the church. Men press very closely to the divine role of the Holy Spirit, the ruler and administrator of Christ's church.

When Christ entered upon His ministry on high, we are told more than a score of times that He "sat down at the right hand of God." Henceforth heaven is His official seat until He returns in power and great glory. He then commissioned the Holy Spirit to rule and to administer in the church, the temple of God, until He returns. There is on earth but one "Holy See," that is, the seat of the Holy One in the church, which only the Spirit of God can occupy without the most daring blasphemy. It requires all true believers to contemplate that picture of one "sitting in the temple of God," and to read the lesson it teaches. We must beware of thrusting any man into the seat of the Holy Spirit, or developing any structural form that encroaches into that sacred place. And let us remember that a democracy may be guilty of the same sin as a hierarchy, in settling solemn issues by show of hands instead of prayerfully waiting for the guidance of the Holy Spirit, substituting the voice of a majority for the voice of the Spirit. We concede that the Holy Spirit makes known His will in the voice of believers, as also in the voice of Scripture; but there must be such prayerful sanctifying of the one and such prayerful search of the other that in reaching decisions in the church there may be the same declaration as in the first Christian council: "It seemed good to the Holy Ghost and to us" (Acts 15:28).

In the profound teaching of Second Corinthians 3 we seem to have a hint as to how we hear the voice of the Lord in guiding the affairs of the church. There the administration of the Spirit is distinctly spoken of in contrast with the administration of the law. Its deliverances are written "not with ink, but with the Spirit of the living God; not in tables of stone, but in the fleshly tables of the heart" (v. 3). There must be a sensitive heart wherein this handwriting may be inscribed; an unhindering will through which He may act. "Where the Spirit of the Lord is, there is liberty," it is written in the same passage (v. 17). Liberty is for God to speak and act as He will through us, which results in loyalty; liberty is not for us to act as we desire, which results in lawlessness.

There is something exceedingly telling in the teaching of the Lord's post-ascension gospel, the Revelation, on this point. The epistles to the seven churches we hold, with many of the best commentators, to be a prophetic setting forth of the successive stages of the church's history—its declines and its recoveries, its failures and its repentances, from ascension to advent. And because the bride of Christ is perpetually betrayed into listening to false teachers and surrendering to the guidance of evil counselors, the Lord is constantly admonishing her to heed the voice of her true teacher and guide, the Holy Spirit. How forcibly this admonition is introduced into the great apocalyptic drama! At each stage of the church's backsliding, a voice is heard from heaven, saying, "He that hath an ear, *let him hear what the Spirit saith unto the churches.*" It is the admonition "of him that hath the seven spirits of God," seven times addressed to His church throughout her earthly history, calling her to return from her false guides and misleading teachers, and to listen to the voice of her true Counselor. It's amazing how deaf the church is even when it is clearly written in Scripture.

From this general statement of the administration of the Holy Spirit, let us now descend to the particular acts and offices in which this authority is exercised.

In the Ministry and Government of the Church

Speaking to the elders of Ephesus, Paul says, "Take heed therefore unto yourselves, and to all the flock, over the which the Holy Ghost hath made you overseers, to feed the church of God" (Acts 20:28). In the beginning, bishops or elders were established by the Spirit of God, not by the decision of the people. The office and its incumbent were by direct divine appointment.

We find this clear word in Ephesians 4: "When he ascended up on high, he led captivity captive, and gave gifts
unto men. . . . And he gave some, apostles; and some,
prophets; and some, evangelists; and some, pastors and
teachers; for the perfecting of the saints, for the work of
ministering, for the edifying of the body of Christ" (vv. 8–
12). The ascent of the Lord and the descent of the Spirit
are here seen in their necessary relation. In the one event
Christ took His seat in heaven as "head over all things to
his church"; in the other, the Holy Spirit came down to
begin the work of "building up the body of Christ." Of
course it is the Head who directs the construction of the
body, as being "fitly framed together it groweth into a holy
temple in the Lord," and it is the Holy Spirit who super-
intends this construction, for "we are builded together for
an habitation of God in the Spirit" (Eph. 2:21). Therefore
all the offices through which this work is to be carried on
were appointed by Christ and instituted through the Spirit.
Suppose then that men invent offices which are not named
in the inspired list, and set up in the church an order of
popes and cardinals, archbishops and archdeacons? Not
only does this introduce confusion into the body of Christ,
but it also has pressed in upon the rule of the Holy Spirit.
On the other hand, suppose that we sacredly maintain
those offices of the ministry which have been established
for permanent continuance in the church, and yet fill these
according to our own preference and will. Is this any less
an affront to the Spirit?

Doubtless, the mistakes of God's servants as given in
Scripture are designed for our instruction and admonition. A recorded warning concerning church administration is given in the first chapter of Acts. A vacancy had
occurred in the apostolate. Standing up in the upper room,
among the hundred and twenty, Peter boldly affirmed that
this vacancy must be filled, and of the men who had com-
panied with them during the Lord's earthly ministry, "must
one be ordained to be a witness with us of his resurrection." But the disciples had never had a voice in choosing

apostles. The Lord had done this of His own sovereign will: "Have I not chosen you twelve?" Now He had gone away into heaven, and His Administrator had not yet arrived to enter upon His office work. Surely if the divine order was to be that, having "ascended on high," He was "to give some apostles," it would seem that with the Holy Spirit not yet come, a valid election of an apostle was impossible. But in spite of this, a nomination was made, prayer was offered in which the Lord was asked to indicate which of the candidates He had chosen, and then after a vote had been taken, Matthias was declared elected. Is there any indication that this choice was ever ratified by the Lord? On the contrary, Matthias passes into obscurity from this time, his name never again being mentioned. Some two years subsequent, the Lord calls Saul of Tarsus; he is sealed with His Spirit, and certified by such evident credentials of the divine appointment that he boldly signs himself "Paul, an apostle, *not of men, neither by man, but by Jesus Christ and God the Father*" (Gal. 1:1).

We believe that the original apostolic office has passed away—the qualification of having been a witness of the Lord's resurrection being now impossible. But let us focus on the office of pastor, elder, bishop, or teacher of the flock. The divine plan is that this office should be filled, just as in the beginning, by the appointment of the Holy Spirit. We do not doubt that if there is a prayerful waiting upon Him for guidance and a sanctified submission to His will when it is made known, He will now choose pastors and set them over their appointed flocks just as manifestly as He did in the beginning.

Very descriptive is the picture in Revelation of the glorified Lord, moving among the candlesticks. There are "seven golden candlesticks" (1:12) now, not one only as in the Jewish temple. The church of God is manifold, not a unit.[1] He who "walketh in the midst of the seven golden

---

[1]By the candlesticks being seven instead of one, as in the tabernacle, we are taught that whereas in the Jewish dispensation, God's visible church was one, in the Gentile dispensation there are many visible churches; and that Christ himself recognizes them alike. *Commentary on the Revelation*, Canon Garratt, p. 32.

candlesticks" "holdeth the seven stars in his right hand"
(1:16). These stars are "the angels of the seven churches"
(1:20)—their ministers or bishops as generally understood. The Lord holds them in His right hand. Does He
not require us to ask of Him alone for their bestowal? Yes.
"Pray ye therefore the Lord of the harvest, that he would
send forth laborers into his harvest" (Luke 10:2). There is
no intimation in Scripture that we are to apply anywhere
but to Him for the ministry of His church. Does He not
give such ministry, and He alone? Yes, for "he gave some
. . . pastors and teachers." And now (Rev. 2:1–7), speaking
to the church in Ephesus, the elders of which Paul had so
affectionately exhorted, He is seen in the position of Chief
Shepherd and Bishop—giving pastors with His own hand;
placing them with His own right hand and warning the
church that though they have tried and rejected false apostles, they have nevertheless left their "first love." Significant word! On this love our Lord conditioned the indwelling of the Father and of the Son through the Holy Spirit
(John 14:23). Losing this the peril becomes imminent that
the candlestick may be removed out of its place; and so
the warning is solemnly announced: "He that hath an ear,
let him hear what the Spirit saith unto the churches."
Without the Spirit the candlestick can shed forth no light,
and loses its place of testimony.

Dead churches, whose witness has been silenced, whose
place has been vacated, even though the lifeless form remains, are we not acquainted with such? The safeguard
against them is found in the Apostle's warning: "Quench
not the Spirit." The voice of the Lord must be heard in His
church, and the Holy Spirit alone has the prerogative of
communicating that voice. Since when was the church under the direction of the state or archbishops or any human
authority? We may congratulate ourselves that we are neither in a State Church nor under an episcopal bishop; but
there are methods of ignoring or repressing the voice of
the Holy Spirit which though simpler and far less apparent are no less violent. The humble and godly membership

of a church may turn to some pastor after much prayer and waiting on God for the Spirit's guidance and the signs of the divine choice may be clearly manifest; yet a pulpit committee, or some conclave of "leading brethren," may veto their action on the ground, perchance, that the candidate is not popular and will not draw. Alas! for the flock so lorded over that the voice of the Holy Spirit cannot be heard.

And majorities are no more to be depended upon than minorities if there is in either case a neglect of patient and prolonged waiting upon the Lord to know His will. Of what value is a show of hands unless His are stretched out "who holdeth the seven stars in his right hand"? One may object that we are holding up an ideal impossible to realize. It is a difficult ideal we admit, as the highest attainments are always difficult, but it is not an impossible one. It is easier to recite our prayers from a book than to "worship in Spirit and in truth" from a prepared heart. It is easier to get "the sense of the meeting" in choosing a pastor than to learn "the mind of the Spirit" by patient waiting and humble surrender to God. But the more laborious way will certainly prove the more profitable way.

The failure to take this way is the cause of more decay and spiritual death in the churches than we have yet imagined. Scores of churches bear the marks of "Ichabod," the glory long since departed. They were founded in prayer and consecration, but their light has been extinguished. Only the lampstand which once bore it still remains, adorned and beautified with all that the highest art and architecture can suggest. Their history is known to Him who walks among the golden candlesticks. What violence and rejection may have been done to Him who is called "the Spirit of counsel and might"? What refusal of the truth which He, "the Spirit of truth," has appointed for the faith of God's church till at last the word has been spoken: "Ye do always resist the Holy Ghost; as your fathers did, so do ye." Is it only Jewish worshipers to whom these words apply? Is it only a Jewish temple of which this sentence is true, "Behold your house is left unto you desolate"? The Spirit will not be entirely withdrawn from the body of Christ indeed, but there is the Church, and there are churches. A man may yet live and breathe when cell after cell has been closed by congestion till at last he only inhales and exhales with a little portion of one lung. Let him that reads understand.

The Spirit is the breath of God in the body of His church. Multitudes of churches have so shut out the Spirit from rule and authority and supremacy that the ascended Lord can only say to them, "Thou hast a name that thou livest, and art dead" (Rev. 3:1). So vital and indispensable is the ministry of the Spirit that without it nothing else will avail. Some trust in creeds, and some in ordinances; some suppose that the church's security lies in a sound theology, and others locate it in a primitive simplicity of government and worship, but it lies in none of these, desirable as they are. The body may be in its members perfect and entire, lacking nothing; but if the Spirit has been withdrawn from it, it has changed from a church into a corpse. As one has powerfully stated it: "When the Holy Spirit withdraws . . . he sometimes allows the forms which he has created to remain. The oil is exhausted, but the lamp is still there; prayer is offered and the Bible read; churchgoing is not given up, and to a certain degree the service is enjoyed; in a word religious habits are preserved, and like the corpses found at Pompeii, which were in a perfect state of preservation and in the very position in which death had surprised them, but which were reduced to ashes by contact with the air, so the blast of trial, of temptation, or of final judgment will destroy these spiritual corpses."[2]

In the Worship and Service of the Church

Is there anything, from highest to lowest, that we are called to do in connection with the worship of the church

---

[2]Pastor G.F. Tophel, *The Work of the Holy Spirit in Man*, p. 66.

of which the Holy Spirit is not the appointed agent? Believers are the instruments through which He acts, but they have no function apart from His inspiration and guidance any more than the organ pipe has without the wind, which breathing through it causes it to resound. To make this clear, we will consider the several parts of the service of the church as we are accustomed to participate in it, and observe their relation to the divine Administrator.

1. Preaching is by general consent an important part of the work of the ministry, both for the pastor and for the evangelist. What is its inspiration and authority? We "have preached the gospel unto you *with the Holy Ghost sent down from heaven*" (1 Pet. 1:12) is Peter's description of the apostolic method. And the words direct our thought to the Spirit not as instrumental but as inspiring. "*In the Holy Ghost,*" the words mean literally. The true preacher does not simply use the Spirit; he is used by the Spirit. He speaks as one moving in the element and atmosphere of the Holy Spirit, and mastered by His divine power.

In this fact a sermon differs immeasurably from a speech, and the preacher from the orator. How distinctly Paul emphasizes this contrast in his letter to the Corinthians (1 Cor. 2:4). The sole substance of his preaching he declares to be "Jesus Christ and him crucified," and the sole inspiration of his preaching, the Holy Spirit: "And my speech and my preaching was not with enticing words of man's wisdom, but in demonstration of the Spirit and power." What did good Philip Henry mean by his resolve "to preach Christ crucified in a crucified style"? More perhaps than he thought or knew. "He shall testify of me" is Jesus' saying concerning the promised Paraclete. The Comforter bears witness to the Crucified. No other theme in the pulpit can be sure of commanding His cooperation.

Philosophy, poetry, art, literature, sociology, ethics, and history are attractive subjects to many minds, and they who handle such themes in the pulpit may set them forth with alluring words of human genius; but there is no certainty that the Holy Spirit will accompany their presentation with His divine attestation. The preaching of the cross, in chastened simplicity of speech, has the demonstration of the Spirit pledged to it, as no secular, or moral, or even formal religious discourse has. From Paul's words to the Thessalonians, "Our gospel came not unto you in word only, but also *in power, and in the Holy Ghost, and in much assurance*" (1 Thess. 1:5), we need to be reminded that "our gospel" meant only one thing to Paul: setting forth Jesus Christ crucified in the midst of the people. Here is the secret of evangelical power. It therefore ought to be the supreme aim of the preacher to use themes that can assuredly command the witness of the Holy Spirit, not seeking topics that will enlist the attention of the people.

Let us set the popular preacher and the apostolic preacher side by side, and consider whose reward we would choose: universal admiration or "God also bearing them witness, both with signs and wonders, and with divers miracles, and *gifts of the Holy Ghost*, according to his will" (Heb. 2:4)?; the sermon greeted with applause and the clapping of hands or "*having received the word with joy of the Holy Ghost*" (1 Thess. 1:6)?; admiration of the preacher captivating all who listen to the discourse or "*the Holy Ghost fell on all them which heard the word*" (Acts 10:44)? Language cannot express the peril involved in this. Our generation is rapidly losing its grip upon the supernatural; and as a consequence the pulpit is rapidly dropping to the level of the platform. And this decline is due, more than anything else, to ignoring the Holy Spirit as the supreme inspirer of preaching. We would rather see a great orator in the pulpit, forgetting that the least expounder of the Word, when filled with the Holy Spirit, is greater than he. We want the convenient gospel; but not in the strenuous gospel set forth by the "Spirit of God."

In all that we have said, we do not ignore the human element in preaching, nor underscore a good education and sanctified mental training. We only emphasize the extreme peril of making that supreme which God has made subordinate. As genius raises the great painter or poet far

above the common man, so it is the Holy Spirit who lifts
the preacher far above the man of genius. The preacher
who brought three thousand to believe on a crucified Christ
under a single sermon anticipated the question of those
who, with an eye upon the mere human accessories of his
sermon, might ask after the secret of his power; and he
unfolds that secret in a single terse sentence: "With the
Holy Ghost sent down from heaven."

2. Prayer is another vital element in the worship of
God's church. "Lord, teach us how to pray, as John also
taught his disciples." Jesus complied literally with this
request of His followers. As John, under the law, could
only give rules and rudiments, not yet having come to the
dispensation of the Spirit, so did Jesus give a form of prayer,
a lesson in the "technique of worship." But when He arrived at the eve of His passion, when He announced the
coming of the Comforter, He led His disciples into the
heart and mystery of the great theme, teaching them to
pray as John *could not* have taught his disciples. "Hitherto
have ye asked nothing in my name," said Jesus (John
16:24). But now that He was about to enter into His me-
diatorial office at God's right hand, and to send forth the
Comforter into the midst of His disciples, this joyful privilege was to be accorded to him: "Whatsoever ye shall ask
the Father *in my name*, he will give it you"[3] (John 16:23).
The words are equivalent to "*in me*." The thought is surely
not that of using the name of Jesus as a password, but
that of entering into His person and appropriating His
will; so that when we pray, it shall be as though Jesus
himself stood in God's presence and made intercession.
Nor is it "as though"—it is the literal fact. We become
identified with Christ through the Spirit, and His will is
accomplished within us by the Holy Spirit, so that to ask
what we desire of Him is to ask what He desires for us.
We are inwilled by His will because we are inspired by

---

[3]It was impossible up to the time of the glorification of Jesus to pray to
the Father in His name. It is a fullness of joy peculiar to the dispensation
of the Spirit to be able to do so. (Alford)

His Spirit, who lives and breathes within us. Therefore we may know that we are always heard, since we are in Him who can boldly say to the Father, "I know that thou always hearest me." It is Christ's mediatorship with the Father, and the Holy Spirit's mediatorship with us, that gives us this high privilege of praying in the name of Jesus, as it is written: "For through him we both have access *in one Spirit* unto the Father."

When we read of "praying always with all prayer and supplication *in the Spirit*" (Eph. 6:18), and of "praying *in the Holy Ghost*" (Jude 20), it is simply an admonition to use our privilege of asking in the name of Jesus. For to be in the Spirit is to be in Christ, united to His person, identified with His will, invested with His righteousness, so that we are as He is before the Father.

In that fullest exposition of the doctrine of the Spirit, given in Romans 8, we see clearly that the ministry of the Comforter consists in His effectuating in us that which Christ is accomplishing for us on the throne. Especially is this true of prayer. In the Epistle to the Hebrews we read: "Wherefore he is able also to save them to the uttermost that come unto God by him, *seeing he ever liveth to make intercession for them*" (Heb. 7:25). In the Epistle to the Romans we read: "Likewise the Spirit also helpeth our infirmities; for we know not what we should pray for as we ought: but *the Spirit itself maketh intercession for us* with groanings which cannot be uttered; and he that searcheth the hearts knoweth what is the mind of the Spirit, because he maketh intercession for the saints according to the will of God" (Rom. 8:26). These passages, read together, clearly show the Spirit doing the same thing *in* us that Christ in heaven is doing *for* us. And, moreover, they reveal to us the method of the glorified Christ in helping those who know not how to pray, teaching them, not by an outward form, but by an inward guidance. Indeed, the prayer inspired by the Holy Spirit is often so deep that it cannot be expressed in formal words, but reaches the ear of the Father only in unspeakable yearnings, in unuttered groanings.

The keynote of all true intercession is the will of God. In the disciples' prayer, as taught them by the Master, this note is distinctly sounded: "Thy will be done on earth as in heaven." In the Savior's garden prayer it is heard again, as with strong crying and tears the Son of God exclaims, "Not my will but thine be done," and in the revelation of the doctrine of prayer through an inspired apostle we read: "If we ask anything according to his will, he heareth us." It is the Spirit's deepest work in the believer to tune his mind to this exalted key, as He "maketh intercession for the saints *according to the will of God.*"

There is a promise which all disciples love to quote for their assurance in prayer: "If two of you shall agree on earth as touching any thing that they shall ask, it shall be done for them of my Father which is in heaven" (Matt 18:19). The word translated "agree" is a very suggestive one. It is the word from which our word "symphony" comes. If two shall *accord* or *symphonize* in what they ask, they have the promise of being heard. But, as in tuning an organ all the notes must be keyed to the standard pitch or else harmony is impossible, so in prayer. It is not enough that two disciples agree with each other; they must both accord with a third, the righteous and holy Lord, before in the scriptural sense they can agree in intercession. Two may agree in most sinful conflict with the divine will: "How is it that ye have *agreed together* [the same word] to tempt the Spirit of the Lord?" asks Peter (Acts 5:9). Here is mutual accord, but guilty discord with the Holy Spirit. It is the Spirit's ministry to tune our wills to the divine; then only can there be praying in the Holy Spirit.

We cannot therefore overemphasize the administration of the Spirit in directing the worship of God's house. The use of liturgical forms is a relapse into legalism, a consent to be taught to pray as "John taught his disciples." True, there may be extemporaneous forms as well as written forms, praying by memory as well as praying by the book. Against both we simply interpose the teaching of the Spirit in which the Father seeks worshipers who "wor-

ship in Spirit and in truth." To pray correctly is the highest of all attainments. The secret lies in a heart that pre-
vails with God because it has been prevailed over by God.
"O Lord," says a saint, "my spirit was like a harp this
morning, making melody before you since you first tuned
the instrument by the Holy Spirit, and then chose the
psalm of praise to be played thereon." Most solemn and
revealing words these have always seemed: "The Father
seeketh such to worship him." Amid all the repetition of
forms and the chanting of liturgies, how earnestly the
Most High searches after the spiritual worshiper, with a
heart in surrender before God, with a spirit so sensitive
to the hidden motions of the Holy Spirit that when the
lips speak they shall utter the effectual inwrought prayer
that availeth much!

Many will say this is impractical and beyond the reach
of the common saint. Yet, we were not speaking of pulpit
prayers especially, in what we have said. The universal
priesthood of believers, which the Scriptures so plainly
teach, constitutes the ground for common intercession, for
"the praying one for another" that is the distinctive feature of the Spirit's administration. The prayer meeting,
therefore, in which the whole body of believers partici-
pates probably comes nearer the pattern of primitive
Christian worship than any other service which we hold.
To apply our principle here, then, what method is found
most satisfactory? Shall the service be arranged beforehand, this one selected to pray, and that one to exhort;
and during the progress of the worship, shall such a one
be called up to lead the devotions, and such a one to follow?
After many years of experience, one can bear emphatic
testimony to the value of another way—that of magnify-
ing the office of the Holy Spirit as the leader of the service,
and of so withholding the pressure of human hands in the
assembly that the Spirit shall have the utmost freedom to
move this one to pray and that one to witness, this one to
sing and that one "to say amen at our giving of thanks,"
according to His own sovereign will. Here we speak not

theoretically but experientially. The fervor and spirituality and sweet naturalness of the latter method has been demonstrated beyond a doubt. Our place is to honor the Holy Spirit as Master of our meetings; to study much the secret of surrender to Him; to cultivate a quick ear for hearing His inward voice and a ready tongue for speaking His audible witness; to submissively keep silent when He forbids as well as to speak when He commands, and we shall learn how much better is God's way of conducting the worship of His house than man's way.[4]

3. The ministry of music in the church is another element of worship whose relation to the Spirit needs to be strongly emphasized. Spiritual singing has a divinely appointed place in the church of Christ. Church music, in the conventional sense of that phrase, has no such place, but is a human invention which custom has in many places been elevated into an ordinance. We often quote the exhortation of the Apostle: "Be filled with the Spirit," without marking the practical service with which this fullness stands immediately connected: "Speaking to yourselves in psalms and hymns and spiritual songs, singing and making melody in your heart to the Lord" (Eph. 5:19). As immediately as prayer is connected with the Holy Spirit in this same epistle: "Praying at all seasons *in the Spirit*," and our edification in the church: "Builded together . . . *through the Spirit*" (Eph. 2:22); and our spiritual energizing: "Strengthened with might *by his Spirit*" (Eph. 3:16); and our approach to God, "Access *by one Spirit* unto the Father" (2:18), so intimately is the worship of praise here connected with the Holy Spirit and made dependent on His power. Therefore it would seem too obvious to need

---

[4]It were well for us to give more heed to the voice of Christian history as related to such questions as these. The rise of "sporadic sects" like the "Quietists," the "Mystics," the "Friends," and the "Brethren," with their emphasis on "the still voice" and "the inward leading," is very suggestive. If we may not go so far as some of these go in the insistence on speaking only as sensibly moved by the Spirit, we may be admonished of the hard, artificial man-made worship which made their protest necessary.

explaining that an unbeliever is disqualified from ministering in the service of song in God's house. Scripturally
this seems incontestable, and yet there is no custom which
has brought a sorer blight upon the life of the church or
a heavier repression upon its spiritual energy than the
habit of introducing unsanctified, unconverted, and even
notoriously worldly persons into the choirs of the churches.

Now the teaching of the text just cited is not only decisive against such performers, but against the choirs
themselves, if the choir's position is that of entertaining
the congregation. Observe how distinctly the mutual and
intercongregational character of Christian singing is here
pointed out: "Speaking *to yourselves* in psalms and hymns
and spiritual songs." The one feature that distinguishes
the worship of the church from that of the temple is that
it is mutual. Under the law there were priests and Levites
to minister and people to be ministered to. But under the
gospel there is a universal spiritual priesthood in which
all minister and all are ministered to. Every act of service
belonging to the Christian church is so described: "Pray
one for another" (James 5:16); "Confess your faults *one to
another*" (James 5:16); "Exhort *one another*" (Heb. 3:13);
Love *one another*" (1 Pet. 1:22); "Bear ye *one another's*
burdens" (Gal. 6:2); "Comfort *one another*" (1 Thess. 4:18).
So with the worship of song. Its reciprocal character is
emphasized, not only in the passage just quoted, but also
in Colossians 3: "Teaching and admonishing *one another*
in psalms and hymns and spiritual songs" (v. 16). This is
according to the clearly defined working of the Spirit. He
establishes our fellowship with the Head of the church,
and through Him with one another. All blessing in the
body is mutual, and the worship ordained to maintain and
increase that blessing is likewise mutual.

Being the inspirer and director of the worship of God's
church, the Spirit must have those who have been renewed
and are indwelt by himself as the instruments through
whom He acts—all others are disqualified. This is shown
even in the types and symbols of the old dispensation. The

holy anointing authorized for Aaron and his sons is confessedly a type of the unction of the Holy Spirit. Mark the rigid and sacred limitations in its use: "Thou shalt anoint Aaron and his sons, and consecrate them, that they may minister unto me in the priest's office. And thou shalt speak unto the children of Israel, saying, This shall be a holy anointing oil unto me throughout your generations. Upon man's flesh it shall not be poured, neither shall ye make any other like it, after the composition of it: it is holy, and it shall be holy unto you. Whosoever compoundeth any like it, or whosoever putteth any of it upon a stranger, shall even be cut off from his people" (Ex. 30:30–33).

Now, of these minute directions we may say confidently that "these things happened unto them for ensamples: and they are written for our admonition, upon whom the ends of the world [ages] are come" (1 Cor. 10:11). The three rigid prohibitions named here touch exactly the errors that are most characteristic of this generation. *"Upon man's flesh it shall not be poured"*—honoring the natural man, and exalting human nature into that place which belongs only to the regenerate. *"Whosoever putteth any of it upon a stranger"*—the sin of thrusting into the ministry and service of the church persons who have never by the new birth been brought into the family of God. *"Whosoever compoundeth any like it"*—the artificial imitation of the Spirit's offices and ministration. Let the Christian reader pause to meditate on these and to be warned.

Many desire the gifts of the Spirit who care little for the Spirit himself. Inspirational music is greatly coveted. So why not buy the very best? Bring in those singers and musicians who will thrill the church and draw to the church those who could not be drawn by the plain attractions of the cross. But what is the exhortation of Scripture? "By him therefore let us offer the sacrifice of praise to God continually, that is, the fruit of our lips giving thanks to his name" (Heb. 13:15). This kind of sacrifice costs—earnest prayer, deep communion, and the fullness of the Spirit.

No sum of money can purchase this and no musician is ingenious enough to imitate it.

What can be said to those churches which spend thousands of dollars yearly in music budgets? This lavish expenditure on artificial worship is almost always accompanied with meager giving for the carrying out of the Great Commission. Shall we purchase what is false to rob God with the other hand? The ministry of song has been committed to the church alone, and to the church under the guidance of the Holy Spirit. Some of her number may be appointed to lead this service, if they themselves are under the leadership of the Spirit. But the church cannot commit this divine ministry to the unsanctified without affronting the Spirit of God and serious peril to her own communion with God.

If in this area we are again accused of setting up an impossible ideal, let the voice of experience be heard as evidence. Let pastors be called to testify of the added blessing and fervor coming to their churches when this ideal has been approximately realized. Compare times of apostasy when the ministry of song was driven into some narrow stall of the church and controlled by a few trained monopolists of worship with eras of revival, of the bursting of the barriers and the people of God seizing once more their defrauded heritage and breaking forth, a great multitude, into "hallelujahs of the heart." Let history speak for itself—the breaking forth in worship of the Lollards and Lutherans, the Wesleyans and Salvationists.

In the Missionary Enterprise of the Church

In the Gospels, which contain the story of Christ's earthly life, we have the record of the giving of the Great Commission: "Go ye into all the world, and preach the gospel to every creature" (Mark 16:15). In the Acts, which contains the story of the life of the Spirit, we have the promise of the coming of the Executor of that Commission: "But ye shall receive power, after that the Holy Ghost is come upon you: and ye shall be witnesses unto me both in Jerusalem, and in Judea, and in Samaria, and unto the uttermost part of the earth" (Acts 1:8). Nowhere is the hand of the Spirit more distinctly seen than in the inauguration and direction of missions. The field is the world, the sower is the disciple, and the seed is the Word. The world can only be touched through the Spirit—"When he is come he will convict the world of sin"; the sower is energized only through the Spirit—"Ye shall receive the power of the Holy Ghost coming upon you"; and the seed is only made productive through the quickening of the Spirit—"He that soweth to the Spirit shall of the Spirit reap life everlasting" (Gal. 6:8). In the simple story of the first mission (Acts. 13), we see how every step in the enterprise was originated and directed by the presiding Spirit.

We observe this:

(1) In the selection of missionaries: "The *Holy Ghost* said, Separate me Barnabas and Saul for the work whereunto I have called them" (13:2).

(2) In their thrusting forth into the field: "So they, being sent forth by the *Holy Ghost*, departed unto Seleucia" (13:4).

(3) In empowering them to speak: "Then Saul, who also is called Paul, filled with the *Holy Ghost*, said" (13:9).

(4) In sustaining them in persecution: "And the disciples were filled with joy, and with the *Holy Ghost*" (13:52).

(5) In setting the divine seal upon their ministry among the Gentiles: "And God, which knoweth the hearts, bare them witness, giving them the *Holy Ghost*, even as he did unto us" (15:8).

(6) In counseling in difficult questions of missionary policy: "It seemed good to the *Holy Ghost*, and to us" (15:28).

(7) In restraining the missionaries from entering into fields not yet appointed by the Lord: They "were forbidden of the *Holy Ghost* to preach the word in Asia. . . . They tried to go into Bithynia: but the *Spirit* permitted them not" (16:6, 7).

Very striking in this record is the ever-present, unfailing, and minute direction of the Holy Spirit in all the steps of this divine enterprise. "But this was in apostolic days," it will be said. Yes, but the promise of the Spirit is that "he shall abide with you for the age." *Unless the age has ended, He is still here, still in office, and still entrusted with the responsibility of carrying out that work dearest to the heart of our glorified Lord.* Who would dare say that we need not return to the first methods and to a resumption of the church's first endowments? The Holy Spirit has not changed, but the church looks elsewhere. If the church trusted less in human wisdom and calculating methods, if she administered less by mechanical rules and recognized that the supernatural work to which she is called is accompanied by a supernatural power, who can doubt that the grinding and groaning of our cumbrous missionary machinery would be vastly decreased and the demonstration of the Spirit far more apparent?

"Have you visited the Cathedral of Freyburg, and listened to that wonderful organist, who with such enchantment draws the tears from the traveler's eyes while he touches, one after another, his wonderful keys, and makes you hear by turns the march of armies upon the beach, or the chanted prayer upon the lake during the tempest, or the voices of praise after it is calm? Well, thus the Eternal God, embracing at a glance the keyboard of sixty centuries, touches by turns, with the fingers of his Spirit, the keys which he had chosen for the unity of his celestial hymn. He lays his left hand upon Enoch, the seventh from Adam, and his right hand on John, the humble and sublime prisoner of Patmos. From the one the strain is heard: 'Behold the Lord cometh with ten thousand of his saints'; from the other: 'Behold he cometh with clouds.' And between the notes of this hymn of three thousand years there is eternal harmony, and the angels stoop to listen, the elect of God are moved, and eternal life descends into men's souls."

—Gaussen's Theopneustia

8

The Inspiration of the Spirit

It is generally held among evangelicals that the order of apostles ceased with the death of those who had seen the Lord and accompanied Him until the day of His ascension. But the reason for this cessation is seldom considered. May we not believe that the apostles and their companions were commissioned to speak authoritatively for the Lord until the New Testament Scriptures should be completed? Historically, at least, it seems to have been the fact, that as the apostles of the new dispensation disappeared, the Gospels and epistles took their place, and that henceforth the divine authoritative voice of the Spirit could be distinctly recognized only in the written word. As coal has been called "fossil sunlight," so the New Testament may be called fossil inspiration, the supernatural illumination which fell upon the apostles being herein stored up for the use of the church throughout the ages.[1]

---

[1]The proof that the inspiration of the apostles and scribes of the New Testament was not transmitted to successors is thus stated by Neander: "A phenomenon singular in its kind is the striking difference between the writings of the apostles and those of the apostolic fathers, so nearly their contemporaries. In other instances transitions are wont to be gradual, but in this instance we observe a sudden change. There is no gentle graduation here, but all at once an abrupt transition from one style of language to another—a phenomenon which should lead us to acknowledge the fact of a special agency of the Divine Spirit in the souls of the apostles and of a new creative element in the first period." (*Church History*, II., 405.)

Inspiration signifies "in breathing." "All scripture is given by inspiration of God [God-breathed], and is profitable for doctrine, for reproof, for correction, for instruction in righteousness" (2 Tim. 3:16). As the Lord breathed the Spirit into certain men, so He breathed His Spirit into certain books and endowed them with his infallibility in teaching truth. God did not choose to inspire all good books, though He has chosen to inbreathe one book, thereby separating it and setting it apart from all other books. The phrase, "the Bible is simply literature," as a suggestion against the divine inspiration of Scripture, is absolutely false. Literature is the letter; Scripture is the letter inspired by the Spirit. What Jesus said in justification of His doctrine of the new birth is equally applicable to the doctrine of inspiration: "That which is born of the flesh is flesh, and that which is born of the Spirit is spirit." Educate, develop, and refine the natural man to the highest possible point, and yet he is far from being a spiritual man. So of literature: however elevated its tone, however lofty its thought, it is not Scripture. Scripture is literature indwelt by the Spirit of God. The absence of the Holy Spirit from all other writing constitutes the impassable gulf between it and Scripture.

Our Lord, speaking about His own doctrine, uses the same language to show its separateness from the common teaching of the day. He says, "It is the Spirit that quickeneth; the flesh profiteth nothing; *the words that I speak unto you, they are spirit, and they are life*" (John 6:63). Words they were, and in that respect, literature, but also words divinely inbreathed and therefore Scripture. The one fact that makes the Word of God a unique book is the indwelling of the Holy Spirit. Therefore we may truly say of the Bible, not merely that it *was* inspired, but it *is* inspired. The Holy Spirit breathes within it, making it not only authoritative in its doctrine but life-giving in its substance, so that they who receive its promises by faith have been "born again, not of corruptible seed, but of incorruptible, through the word of God, which liveth and abideth forever" (1 Pet. 1:23).

Thus far we have been concerned with the various works and offices of the Paraclete. Here we desire to consider that the Holy Spirit not only acts but speaks. Listen to the repeated affirmations of this fact. Seven times our glorified Lord says, speaking in the Apocalypse: "He that hath an ear, let him hear what *the Spirit saith* unto the churches" (Rev. 2:7). The Paraclete on earth answers to the Paraclete above, so that to the voice from heaven saying, "Write, blessed are the dead which die in the Lord from henceforth," the response is heard: "Yea, *saith the Spirit*, that they may rest from their labors" (Rev. 14:13). This accords with the general tenor of Scripture as to its own Author. In referring to the Old Testament, Peter says, "This scripture must needs have been fulfilled, which *the Holy Ghost by the mouth of David spake* before concerning Judas, which was guide to them that took Jesus" (Acts 1:16). And again: "David himself *said by the Holy Ghost*" (Mark 12:36), our Lord thus plainly recognizing the voice of the Spirit in the voice of the psalmist. So again: "*The Spirit of the Lord spake by me*, and his word was in my tongue. The God of Israel said, the Rock of Israel spake to me" (2 Sam. 23:2, 3), and "Wherefore as *the Holy Ghost saith*, today if ye will hear his voice" (Heb. 3:7).

And what is it to speak? Is it not to express thought in language? The difference between thinking and saying is simply the difference of words. Therefore, if the Holy Spirit "*saith*," we are to find in the *words* of Scripture the exact substance of what He saith. Hence verbal inspiration seems absolutely essential for conveying to us the exact thought of God. And while many are inclined to ridicule the idea as mechanical, the conduct and method of scholars of every shade of belief show how generally it is accepted. This is seen in the minute study of the *words* of Scripture carried on by all expositors, their search after the precise shade of verbal significance, their attention to the minutest details of language and to all the delicate coloring of mood and tense and accent. The higher critics who speak lightly of the theory of literal inspiration by their method of study and exegesis give the strongest affirmation to the doctrine which they deny. They know that language is the expression of thought. Words determine the size and shape of ideas. As exactly as the coin answers to the die in which it is struck does the thought answer to the word by which it is uttered. Vary the language by the slightest modification, and you by so much vary the thought.

To deny that it is the Holy Spirit who speaks in Scripture is an intelligible position; but admitting that *He speaks*, we can only understand His thoughts by listening to His words. True, He may move within us emotions too deep for expression, as when "the Spirit itself maketh intercession for us with groanings which cannot be uttered" (Rom. 8:26). But the idea which is really intelligible is the idea that is embodied in speech. For finite minds, at least, words are the measure of comprehensible thoughts. Evidently Jesus claims for His teaching not only inspiration, but verbal inspiration, when He says that His *words* are "spirit and life." And to this agrees the saying of Paul, in speaking of the inspiration of the Holy Spirit: "but God hath revealed them unto us by his Spirit: for the Spirit searcheth all things, yea, the deep things of God. For what man knoweth the things of man, save the spirit of man which is in him? even so the things of God knoweth no man, but the Spirit of God. Now we have received, not the spirit of the world, but the Spirit which is of God, that we might know the things which are freely given to us of God. Which things also we speak, *not in the words which man's wisdom teacheth, but which the Holy Ghost teacheth*; comparing spiritual things with spiritual" (1 Cor. 2:10–13).

And what if one objects that this theory makes inspiration purely mechanical, turning the writers of Scripture into stenographers whose office is simply to transcribe the words of the Spirit as they are dictated? It must be confessed that there is much in Scripture to support this view of the case. This appears to be the exact picture of what we have in the following passage from Scripture: "Of which

salvation the prophets have inquired and searched diligently, who prophesied of the grace that should come unto
you: *searching what, or what manner of time the Spirit of
Christ which was in them did signify, when it testified
beforehand the sufferings of Christ and the glory that should
follow"* (1 Pet. 1:10, 11). Here were inspired writers, studying the meaning of what they themselves had written. If
they were prophets on the manward side, they were evidently pupils on the Godward side. With all possible al-
lowance for the human characteristics of the writers, they
must have been reporters of what they heard, rather than
the formulators of that which they had been made to understand. How nearly this also describes the attitude of
Christ—a hearer that He might be a teacher: "All things
that I have heard of my Father I have made known unto
you" (John 15:15); a reporter that He might be a revealer:
"I have given unto them *the words* which thou gavest me"
(John 17:8).

In these days scholars are captivated with the human
element in inspiration, but the sovereign element is what
most impresses the diligent student of this subject. Concerning inspiration by the Spirit, the teaching is clear:
"the prophecy came not in old time *by the will of man*: but
holy men of God spake as they were moved by the Holy
Ghost" (2 Pet. 1:21). The style of Scripture is, no doubt,
according to the traits and idiosyncracies of the several
writers; but to say that the thoughts of the Bible are from
the Spirit, and the language from men, creates a dualism
in revelation not easy to justify. The words of an eminent
writer upon this subject are invaluable here: "The opinion
that the subject matter alone of the Bible proceeded from
the Holy Spirit, while its language was left to the unaided
choice of the various writers, amounts to that fantastic
notion which is the grand fallacy of many theories of inspiration; namely, that two spiritual agencies were in operation, one of which produced the phraseology in the outward form, while the other created within the soul the
conceptions and thoughts of which such phraseology was

the expression. The Holy Spirit, on the contrary, as the productive *principle*, embraces the entire activity of those whom He inspires, rendering their language the *word of God*."[2]

If it is urged that the quotations which the New Testament makes from the Old are rarely word for word, the language being in many instances changed, it should be noted in reply how significant even these changes often are. If the Holy Spirit directed in the writing of both books, He would have a sovereign right to alter the phraseology, if need be, from the one to the other. In the opinion of many scholars, the change of "the Redeemer shall come *to* Zion, and unto them that turn from transgressions in Jacob," in Isaiah 59:20, to "There shall come *out* of Zion the Deliverer," in Romans 11:26, is an inspired and intentional change.[3] So of the citation from Amos 9:11: "In that day will I raise up the tabernacle of David that is fallen," as given in Acts 15:16, "After this I will return, and I will build again the tabernacle of David, which is fallen down"; the modification of the language seems designed, in order to make clear its significance in its present setting. Many other examples might be given of a reshaping of His own words by the divine Author of Scripture.

On the other hand, the constant recurrence of the same words and phrases in books of the Bible most widely separated in the time and circumstances of their composition strongly suggests sameness of authorship amid the variety of penmanship. The individuality of the writers was no doubt preserved; this individuality, however, was subordinated to the sovereign individuality of the Holy Spirit. It is with the written word as with the incarnate Word. Because Christ is divine, He is more truly human than any whom the world has ever seen, and because the Bible is supernatural, it is natural as no other book which was ever written. Its divinity lifts it above those faults of style

---

[2]Lee on the *Inspiration of the Holy Scripture*, pp. 32, 33.
[3]See Lange's "Commentary" in loco.

that are the fruits of self-consciousness and ambition. Whether we read the Old Testament story of Abraham's servant seeking a bride for Isaac or the New Testament narrative of the walk of the risen Christ with His disciples to Emmaus, the inimitable simplicity of the diction would make us think that we were listening to the dialect of the angels who never sinned in thought, and therefore cannot sin in style, if we didn't know rather that it is the phraseology of the Holy Spirit.

An eminent German theologian has written a sentence so profoundly significant that we here reproduce it in italics: *"We can in fact speak with good reason of a language of the Holy Ghost. For it lies in the Bible plainly before our eyes, how the Divine Spirit, who is the agent of revelation, has fashioned for himself a quite peculiar religious dialect out of the speech of that people which forms its theatre."*[4] So true do we hold this saying to be that it seems to us quite impossible that the exact meaning of many of the terms of the New Testament Greek should be found in a lexicon of classic Greek. Though the verbal form is the same in both, the inbreathed Spirit may have imparted such new significance to old words that to employ a secular dictionary for translating Scripture is almost like calling an unregenerate man to interpret the mysteries of the regenerate life. Progress and discovery have put new meanings into many English words so that one must be in "the spirit of the age" in order to comprehend them. Thus, even in the work of verbal criticism, it is essential that one possess the Spirit of Christ in order to translate the words of Christ.

As to the question of the "inerrancy of Scripture," as the modern phrase is, we may well pass by many minor arguments and emphasize the one great reason for holding this view: If it is God the Holy Spirit who speaks in Scripture, then the Bible is the word of God, and like God, infallible. A recent writer has challenged us to show where

---

[4]Rothe, *Dogmatics*, p. 238.

the Bible anywhere calls itself "The word of God." The most elementary student of the subject can with a concordance easily point out the passages which so describe it. But we dwell on the fact that it is not only called "*the word of God*," but "*the oracles of God.*" This collective name of the Scriptures is most significant. We need not inquire of the heathen about the meaning they put on the words as the authoritative utterances of their gods; let the usage of Scripture make its own impression: "What advantage then hath the Jew? or what profit is there of circumcision? Much every way: chiefly, because that unto them were committed *the oracles of God*" (Rom. 3:2).[5]

This comprehensive expression is very helpful when critics assail the books of the Old Testament in detail. Here the Holy Spirit authenticates them for us in their entirety—the books of the Law and the Prophets and the Psalms bound together in one bundle of inspired authority. Stephen, in like manner, speaks of his nation as those "who received the *lively oracles* [of God] to give unto us" (Acts 7:38); and Peter says, "If any man speak, let him speak as *the oracles of God*" (1 Pet. 4:11). Moreover, the same apostles who submitted to the authority of the Old Testament as the oracles of God themselves claimed to write as the oracles of God in the New Testament. "If any man," says Paul, "think himself to be a prophet, or spiritual, let him acknowledge that the things that I write unto you are the *commandments of the Lord*" (1 Cor. 14:37). "We are of God," writes John. "He that knoweth God heareth us; he that is not of God heareth not us" (1 John 4:6). These claims are too great to be put forth concerning fallible writings. Admitting their premises, the Jews were right in charging Jesus with blasphemy, in that being a man He made himself God. If Christ is not God, He is not

---

[5]The Apostle in calling the Old Testament Scriptures the "oracles of God," clearly recognizes them as divinely inspired books. The Jewish church was the trustee and guardian of these oracles till the coming of Christ. Now the Scriptures of the Old and New Testament are committed to the guardianship of the Christian church. (Dr. Philip Schaff)

even a good man. And if the Scriptures are not inerrant, they are worse than errant; since, being literature, they make themselves the word of God.

And what if it be said that there are irreconcilable contradictions in this book which calls itself the oracles of God? Two things may be said: First, the Bible is a spiritual book and it should be expected that if examined according to "the scientific method" many difficulties in perception would occur. In the same paragraph in which the Bible claims that its very words are the words of the Holy Spirit, it repudiates the scientific method as futile for the understanding of those words: "Eye hath not seen, nor ear heard"—and insists on the spiritual method as alone adequate—"but God hath revealed them unto us by his Spirit" (1 Cor. 2:9, 10). Not only does the Bible not yield roses to the critic, it yields the thorns and briars of hopeless misperception. Faith and opened spiritual eyes hold not only the keys to all the creeds, but also to many of the contradictions. Second, apparent contradictions have often been resolved through detailed study and more recent archaeological study. There seems to the critic to be historic error in the statement of Stephen that Jacob was buried at Sychem (Acts 7:16) instead of in the field of Machpelah before Mamre, as recorded in Gen. 50:13, just as it was once thought that Luke had made a mistake in his reference to Cyrenious in chapter 2:1, 2. The former contradiction may disappear in the same way as the latter has, confirming the habitual accuracy of Scripture by the investigation the perceived contradiction called forth. And so also with such alleged discrepancies as that between the record in one place that King Solomon had four thousand stalls for horses, and in another forty thousand; or that of the statement in one passage that King Josiah began to reign at eight years of age, and in another at eighteen. What if we freely admit that we cannot reconcile these statements? That does not prove that they are not reconcilable. The history of solved contradictions has certainly shown that as "the foolishness of God is wiser than men, and the weakness of God stronger than men," so the discords of God are more harmonious than men.

We may say, in closing this chapter, that almost the highest proof of the infallibility of Scripture is the practical: we have proved it true. As the coin of the State always has been found able to buy the amount represented on its face, so the prophecies and promises of Holy Scripture have yielded their face value to those who have taken pains to prove them. Certainly multitudes of Christians have so proved the truthfulness of Scripture that they are ready to trust it without reserve in all that it pledges for the world yet unseen and the life yet unrealized. "Believe that thou mayest know," then, is the admonition which Scripture and history combine to enforce. In the farewell of that great saint, Adolph Monod, these golden words occur: "When I shall enter the invisible world, I do not expect to find things different from what the word of God represented them to me here. The voice I shall then hear will be the same I now hear upon the earth, and I shall say, 'This is indeed what God said to me; *and how thankful I am that I did not wait till I had seen in order to believe.'* "

"The Comforter in every part of his threefold work glorifies Christ. In convincing of sin, he convinces us of the sin of not believing on Christ. In convincing us of righteousness, he convinces us of the righteousness of Christ, of that righteousness which was made manifest in Christ going to the Father, and which he received to bestow on all such as should believe in him. And lastly, in convincing of judgment, he convinces us that the prince of the World was judged in the life and by the death of Christ. Thus throughout, Christ is glorified; and that which the Comforter shows to us relates in all its parts to the life and work of the incarnate Son of God."

—Julius Charles Hare

9

The Conviction of the Spirit

"And when he is come *he will reprove the world of sin, and of righteousness, and of judgment*" (John 16:8). Some mistakenly think from this verse that since the day of Pentecost the Spirit has been universally diffused in the world, touching hearts everywhere, among the evangelized and the unevangelized alike, awakening in them a sense of sin. The Lord says in this same discourse concerning the Comforter: "*Whom the world cannot receive, because it seeth him not, neither knoweth him*" (John 14:17). With these words should be associated the limitation which Jesus makes in the gift of the Paraclete: "If I depart I will send him unto *you*." Christ's disciples were to be the recipients of the Holy Spirit and His church the mediator between the Spirit and the world. "And when he is come [to you], he will reprove the world." And to complete the exposition, we may connect this promise with the Great Commission, "Go ye into *all the world* and preach the gospel to every creature," and conclude that when the Lord sends His messengers into the world, the Spirit of truth goes with them, witnessing to the message which they bear, convincing of the sin which they reprove, and revealing the righteousness which they proclaim.

It will help us then in understanding this subject if we consider the Spirit of truth as sent *unto the church*, testifying *of Christ*, and bringing conviction *to the world*.

As there is a threefold work of Christ, as prophet, priest, and king, so there is a corresponding threefold conviction of the Spirit: "And when he is come, he will reprove the world of sin, and of righteousness, and of judgment: of sin, because they believe not on me; of righteousness, because I go to my Father, and ye see me no more; of judgment, because the prince of this world is judged" (John 16:8). This witness of the Spirit concerns the testimony of Christ as He spoke to men during His time on earth, the work of Christ now carried on in His intercession at God's right hand, and the sentence of Christ when He shall come again to be our judge.

Of Sin

Why is He needed for this conviction? Is not conscience present in every person and doing its work so faithfully? We reply: Conscience is the witness to the law; the Spirit is the witness to grace. Conscience brings legal conviction; the Spirit brings evangelical conviction. The one brings a conviction unto despair, the other a conviction unto hope.

"Of sin, because they believe not on me" describes the ground of the Holy Spirit's conviction. The entrance of Christ into the world rendered possible a sin before unknown: "If I had not come and spoken unto them, they had not had sin; but now they have no cloak for their sin" (John 15:22). Evil seems to have required the presence of incarnate goodness in order to fully manifest itself. Hence the deep significance of the prophecy of Jesus: "Behold, this child is set for the fall and rising again of many in Israel; and for a sign which shall be spoken against . . . *that the thoughts of many hearts may be revealed*" (Luke 2:34, 35). All the most hideous sins of human nature came out during the betrayal and trial and passion of our Lord. In that "hour and power of darkness" these sins were scarcely recognized. But when the day of Pentecost had come with its awesome revealing light of the Spirit of truth, then

there was great contrition in Jerusalem—a contrition the sting of which we find in the charge of Peter: "Jesus of Nazareth, whom ye have taken and by wicked hands have crucified and slain." Following the gift of the Spirit, three thousand were brought to repentance in a single day. Was not that deep conviction a conviction of sin because they had not believed on Christ?

For our reproof the Holy Spirit presents another side of the same fact, calling us to repentance for having refused to take part in Christ crucified—for having refused to believe in Him who was "delivered for our offenses and raised again for our justification." Wherever the preaching of the gospel makes known the fact of Christ having died for the sins of the world, this guilt becomes possible. Not believing in Christ is the great sin now, because it summarizes all other sins. He bore for us the penalties of the law, and thus our obligation, which was originally to the law, is transferred to him. To refuse to trust in Him, therefore, is to repudiate the claims of the law which He fulfilled and to repudiate the debt of infinite love which, by His sacrifice, we have incurred. Nevertheless, the Spirit of truth brings home this sin against the Lord, not to condemn the world, but that the world through Him might be saved.

It has been well said, "It is not the sin-question but the Son-question" which we really raise now in preaching the gospel. "Christ having perfectly satisfied God about sin, the question now between God and your heart is: Are you perfectly satisfied with Christ as the alone portion of your soul? Christ has settled every other to the glory of God." In dealing with the guilty Jews, it was the historical fact that the Holy Spirit urged for their conviction: "Ye denied the Holy One and the Just . . . and killed the Prince of life" (Acts 3:14, 15). In dealing with us, it is the theological fact: "Christ also hath once suffered for sins, the just for the unjust, that he might bring us to God" (1 Pet. 3:18). We are condemned when we have not believed on Him and confessed Him as Savior and Lord. In the one case it is the guilt of despising and rejecting the Son of God; in the other, it is the guilt of not believing in Him who was despised and rejected of men. Yet if we submissively yield, the Spirit will lead us from this first stage of revelation to the second.

Of Righteousness

Not until He had been seated in the heavenly places had Christ perfected righteousness for us. As He was "delivered for our offenses and raised again for our justification," so must He be enthroned for our assurance. It is necessary to see Jesus standing at the right hand of God in order to know ourselves "accepted in the Beloved." How beautiful the culmination of Isaiah's passion-prophecy wherein, accompanying the promise that "he shall bear the sin of many," is the prediction that "by his knowledge *shall my righteous servant justify many*"! But He must be shown to be righteous, in order that He may justify; and this is what His exaltation does. Cartwright has well said: "It was the proof that him whom the world condemned, God justified—that the stone which the builders rejected, God made the Headstone of the corner—that him whom the world denied and lifted up on a cross of shame in the midst of two thieves, God accepted and lifted up in the midst of the throne."

The words "and because ye see me no more," perplexing to the commentators, seem to us to give the real clue to the meaning of the whole passage. As long as the high priest was within the veil and unseen, the congregation of Israel could not be sure of their acceptance. Hence the eager anxiety with which they waited his coming out with the assurance that God had received the propitiation offered on their behalf. Christ, our great High Priest, has entered into the Holy of Holies by His own blood: "Who being the brightness of his glory, and the express image of his person, and upholding all things by the word of his power, when he had by himself purged our sins, sat down on the right hand of the Majesty on high" (Heb. 1:3). Until He comes forth again at His second advent, how can we be assured that His sacrifice for us is accepted? We could not be unless He had sent out one from His presence to make known this fact to us. And this is precisely what He has done in the gift of the Holy Spirit. The presence of the Spirit in the midst of the church is proof positive of the presence of Jesus in the midst of the throne; as is said by Peter on the day of Pentecost: "Therefore being by the right hand of God exalted, and having received of the Father the promise of the Holy Ghost, he hath shed forth this, which ye now see and hear" (Acts 2:33).

Now the Lord's words seem clear to us. Because He ascends to the Father, to be seen no more until His second coming, the Spirit now comes down to attest His presence and approval with the Father as the perfectly righteous One. How clearly this comes out in Peter's defense before the Council: "The God of our fathers raised up Jesus, whom ye slew and hanged on a tree. Him hath God exalted with his right hand to be a Prince and a Saviour, for to give repentance to Israel, and forgiveness of sins. And we are his witnesses of these things; *and so is also the Holy Ghost*, whom God hath given to them that obey him" (Acts 5:30–32). Why this twofold witness? The reason is obvious. The disciples could bear testimony to the crucifixion and resurrection of Christ, but not to His enthronement; the Holy Spirit, who had witnessed that fact in heaven, must be sent down as a joint-witness with the apostles that the whole circle of redemption truth might be attested. Therein was the promise of Jesus in His last discourse literally fulfilled: "But when the Comforter is come, whom I will send unto you from the Father, even the Spirit of truth, which proceedeth from the Father, he shall testify of me: and ye also shall bear witness, because ye have been with me from the beginning" (John 15:26, 27).

As we have said, it is not only the enthronement of Christ in righteous approval with the Father that must be certified, but the acceptance of His sacrificial work as a full and satisfying ground of our reconciliation with the Father. And the Spirit proceeding from God is alone competent to bear to us this assurance. Therefore in the Epistle to the Hebrews, after the reiterated statement of our Lord's exaltation at the right hand of God, it is added: "For by one offering he hath perfected forever them that are sanctified. *Whereof the Holy Ghost also is a witness to us*" (Heb. 10:14, 15). In a word, He whom we have known on the cross as "the Lamb of God that taketh away the sins of the world," must now be known to us on the throne as "*the Lord our righteousness*." We are told that "if any man sin we have a *Paraclete* with the Father, Jesus Christ the righteous" (1 John 2:1); but we can only know Christ as such through that "other Paraclete" sent forth from the Father. It was promised that "when he, the Spirit of truth, is come, he . . . shall not speak of himself; but whatsoever He shall hear, that shall he speak" (John 16:13). Hearing the ascriptions of worthiness lifted up to Christ in heaven, the Holy Spirit communicates what He sees and hears to the church on earth. Thus, as He in His earthly life, through His own outshining and self-evidencing perfection, "was justified in the spirit"; so we, recognizing Him standing on our behalf in glory, and now "of God made unto us righteousness," are also "justified in the name of the Lord Jesus, *and by the Spirit of our God*" (1 Cor. 6:11).

Thus, though unseen by the church during the time of His high-priestly ministry, our Lord has sent to His church One whose office it is to bear witness to all He is doing while in heaven. Therefore have "boldness and access with confidence by the faith of him" and come boldly to the throne of grace, "the Holy Ghost this signifying"—what He could not under the old covenant—"that the way into the holiest of all" (Heb. 9:8) has been made manifest.

And yet—strange paradox—in this same discourse in which Jesus speaks to His disciples of seeing Him no more, He says, "Yet a little while, and the world seeth me no more; *but ye see me*; because I live, ye shall live also" (John 14:19); words which by common consent refer to the same

time of Christ's continuance within the veil. But it is now
by the inward vision, which the world has not, that they
are to behold him. And they are to behold Him *for the
world*, since Christ said of Him: "Whom the *world cannot
receive, because* it seeth him not, neither knoweth him."
And yet it is "to *reprove the world*" "of sin and of righteousness and of judgment" that the Spirit was to be sent.
How shall we understand it? When the sun retires beyond
the horizon at night, our hemisphere sees it no more; yet
the moon sees the sun, and all night long reflects its light
down upon us. So the world sees Christ only through the
illumination of the Comforter reflected in the church; as
it is written: "Eye hath not seen nor ear heard, neither
have entered into the heart of man, the things which God
hath prepared for them that love him. *But God hath revealed them unto us by his Spirit*" (1 Cor. 2:9, 10). And the
church, seeing these things, communicates what she sees
to the world. Christ is all and in all, and the Spirit receives
and reflects Him to the world through His people.

Of Judgment

Here, we believe, is a still further advance in the revelation of the gospel, and not a retreat to the doctrine of
a future judgment, as some would teach. For we repeat
our conviction, that in this entire discourse the Holy Spirit
is revealed to us as a messenger of grace, and not as a
sheriff of the law. Hear the Apostle Peter once more as he
points to Jesus: "By him all that believe are justified from
all things, from which ye could not be justified by the law
of Moses" (Acts 13:39). Justification, in the evangelical
sense, is but another name for judgment prejudged and
condemnation ended. In the enthroned Christ every question about sin is answered, and every claim of a violated
law is absolutely met. Because "Christ has become the end
of the law for righteousness to every one that believeth,"
now "*grace reigns through righteousness* unto eternal life
by Jesus Christ our Lord." Notice the paradox set forth by

Isaiah: *"By his stripes we are healed,"* as though it were told us that sin's affliction had procured sin's remission. And so it is. If the Holy Spirit shows us the wounds of the dying Christ for condemning us, He immediately shows us the wounds of the exalted Christ for comforting us. His glorified body is death's certificate of discharge, the law's receipt in full, assuring us that all the penalties of transgression have been endured, and the Sin-bearer acquitted.

The meaning of this last conviction seems plain therefore: *"Of judgment, because the prince of this world is judged."* Recall the words of Jesus as He stood face to face with the cross: "Now is the judgment of this world: now shall the prince of this world be cast out" (John 12:31). "The accuser of the brethren" is at last judged and ejected from court. The death of Christ is the death of death, and of the author of death also: "That through death he might destroy him that had the power of death, that is, the devil; and deliver them who through fear of death were all their lifetime subject to bondage" (Heb. 2:14, 15).

If the relation of Satan to our judgment and condemnation is mysterious, it is yet clear that Christ by His cross has delivered us from His dominion. We must believe that Jesus spoke the literal truth when He said, "Verily, verily, I say unto you, He that heareth my word, and believeth on him that sent me, hath everlasting life, *and shall not come into condemnation,* but is passed from death unto life" (John 5:24). On the cross Christ judged sin and acquitted those who believe on Him, and in heaven He defends them against every re-arrest by a violated law. "There is therefore now no condemnation to them which are in Christ Jesus" (Rom. 8:1).

Thus the threefold conviction brings the sinner the three stages of Christ's redemptive work, past judgment and past condemnation into eternal acceptance with the Father. We have a striking example in Acts of threefold conviction of conscience where the co-witness of the Spirit was not accepted. Paul before Felix "reasoned of *righteous-*

ness, temperance, and judgment to come" (Acts 24:25). Here
the sin of a licentious life was laid bare as the Apostle
discoursed of purity of conduct; the claims of righteousness were vindicated, and the certainty of coming judgment exhibited—all only with the effect that "Felix trem-
bled." So it must ever be under the convictions of
conscience—anxiety without coming to peace. We have
also an instructive contrast exhibited in Scripture, between the co-witness of the Spirit and the co-witness of
conscience. "*The Spirit itself beareth witness* with our spirit,
that we are the children of God" (Rom. 8:16). Here is the
assurance of sonship, with all the divine inward persua-
sion of freedom from condemnation which it carries. On
the other hand is the conviction of the heathen, who have
only the law written in their hearts: "*Their conscience also
bearing witness*, and their thoughts the meanwhile accus-
ing or else excusing one another; in the day when God
shall judge the secrets of men" (Rom. 2:15, 16). Conscience
can "accuse," and how universally it does so. Conscience
can "excuse," which is the method that guilty thoughts
invariably suggest. But *conscience cannot justify*. Only the
Spirit of truth, whom the Father hath sent forth into the
world, can do this. The work of the two witnesses may be
thus set in contrast:

Conscience Convinces—	The Comforter Convinces—
Of sin committed;	Of sin committed;
Of righteousness impossible;	Of righteousness imputed;
Of judgment impending.	Of judgment accomplished.

Fortunately these two witnesses may be harmonized,
and they are by the atonement, which reconciles man to
himself as well as man to God. Very significantly does the
Epistle to the Hebrews make "having our hearts *sprinkled
from an evil conscience*" the condition of our approach to
God. As the high priest carried the blood into the Holy of
Holies in connection with the old dispensation, so does the

Spirit take the blood of Christ into the inner sanctuary of our spirit in the more wondrous economy of the new dispensation, in order that He may "purge your conscience from dead works to serve the living God" (Heb. 9:14). Blessed is the man who is so reconciled that he can say, "I say the truth in Christ, I lie not, *my conscience also bearing me witness in the Holy Ghost*" (Rom. 9:1). The believer's conscience dwelling in the Spirit, even as his life is "hid with Christ in God," both having the same mind and bearing the same testimony—this is the end of redemption and this is the victory of the atoning blood.

"The Apostle Paul evidently saw the redemption of the bodies of the saints and their manifestation as the sons of God and with them the redemption of the whole creation from its present bondage to be the complete harvest of the Spirit, whereof the church doth now possess only the first-fruits, that is, the first ripe grains which could be formed into a sheaf and presented in the temple as a wave-offering unto the Lord. 'That Holy Spirit of Promise which is the earnest of our inheritance,' saith the same apostle—the earnest, like the first-fruit, being only a part of that which is to be earned . . . yet a sufficient surety that the whole shall in the fullness of the times, be likewise ours."

—Edward Irving

10

The Ascent of the Spirit

"He that descended is the same also that ascended up far above all heavens." So writes the Apostle concerning our ascended Lord (Eph. 4:9). And what is true of Christ is true of the Holy Spirit, who was sent down to abide with us during this age. When He has accomplished His temporal mission in the world, He will return to heaven in the body He has fashioned for himself—that "one new man," the regenerate church, gathered out from both Jews and Gentiles during this dispensation. At the rapture of the saints predicted by the Apostle, the earthly Christ will rise to meet the heavenly Christ. At the sound of the trumpet and the resurrection of the righteous dead, "we which are alive and remain shall be caught up together with them in the clouds, to meet the Lord in the air" (1 Thess. 4:17). The elect church will be gathered in the Spirit as one with him in name (1 Cor. 12:12), taken up to be united in glory with Christ, "the Head of the church: and he is the saviour of the body" (Eph. 5:23). In the council at Jerusalem it is announced as the distinctive work of the Spirit in this dispensation "to gather out *a people for his name.*" It was not by accident or as a term of derision that the first believers received their name, but "the disciples were called *Christians* first in Antioch" (Acts 11:26). This was the name preordained for them, that "honorable name"

139

by which they are called (James 2:7).

When this out-gathering is accomplished and *the people for his name* completed, they will be translated to be one with Him in glory, as they were one with Him in name. The Head will take the body to himself (Eph. 5:29). And this translation of the church is to be accomplished by the Holy Spirit who dwells in her. "But if the Spirit of him that raised up Jesus from the dead dwell in you, he that raised up Christ from the dead shall also quicken your mortal bodies by his Spirit that dwelleth in you" (Rom 8:11). It is not by acting upon the body of Christ from without but by energizing it from within that the Holy Spirit will effect the body's glorification. In a word, the Comforter, who on the day of Pentecost came down to form a body out of flesh, will at the *Parousia* return to heaven in that body. He will have fashioned it into the body of Christ so it may be presented to him "not having spot, or wrinkle, or any such thing . . . holy and without blemish" (Eph. 5:27).

It is necessary to understand this future role of the Holy Spirit. Elder Cumming makes this remark, so striking and yet so true: "*As Christ shall ultimately give up his kingdom to the Father (1 Cor. 15:24–28), so the Holy Ghost shall give up his administration to the Son, when he comes in glory and all his holy angels with him.*" The church and the kingdom are not identical terms, if we mean by the kingdom the visible reign and government of Jesus Christ on earth. But in another sense they are identical. As the King, so the kingdom. The King is present now in the world, only invisibly and by the Holy Spirit. Likewise the kingdom is now present invisibly and spiritually in the hearts of believers. The King is to come again visibly and gloriously, and so shall the kingdom appear visibly and gloriously. In other words, the kingdom is already here in mystery; then it will be here in manifestation. Now the spiritual kingdom is administered by the Holy Spirit, and it extends from Pentecost to *Parousia*. At the *Parousia*—the appearing of the Son of Man in glory—He shall take unto himself His great power and reign (Rev. 11:17). He who has gone to a far country to be invested with a kingdom shall return and enter upon His government (Luke 19:15). Then the invisible shall give way to the visible, the kingdom in mystery shall emerge into the kingdom in manifestation, and the Holy Spirit's administration shall yield to that of Christ.

Here our discussion properly ends, since the age-ministry of the Holy Spirit terminates with the return of Jesus Christ in glory. But there is a "world to come" (Heb. 6:5), succeeding "this present evil world" (Gal. 1:4). We may, in closing, take a glimpse at that next age for the light which it may throw upon the present dispensation.

What significance has the phrase, *"the firstfruits of the Spirit,"* which occurs several times in the New Testament? The firstfruits is but a handful compared with the whole harvest, and this is what we have in the gift of the "Holy Spirit of promise, *which is the earnest of our inheritance until the redemption of the purchased possession"* (Eph. 1:13, 14). The harvest, to which all the firstfruits look forward, is at the appearing of the Lord. Christ, by His rising from the dead, became "the first-fruits of "them that slept" (1 Cor. 15:20). The full harvest, of course, is at the advent, when "they that are Christ's at his coming" shall be raised up (1 Cor. 15:23). So of the Holy Spirit. We all have the Spirit, but not *all* of the Spirit. As a person of the Godhead, He is here in His entirety; but as to His ministry, we have as yet but a part or earnest of His full blessing. To make this statement clear, let us observe that the work of the Holy Spirit during this entire dispensation is elective. He gathers from Jew and Gentile the body of Christ, the *ecclesia*, the called-out. This is His peculiar work in this gospel age. The present is the age of election, and not of universal in-gathering.

But is this all we have to hope for? Let the Word of God answer. Paul, in considering the hope of Israel, says that there is at this present time "a *remnant according to the election of grace*." A little further on he declares in connection with the coming of the Deliverer that *"all Israel shall be saved"* (Rom. 11:5, 26). Now is an elective out-gathering, and then a universal in-gathering, or, as the Apostle sums it up in this same chapter: "If the first-fruits be holy, so also the lump." On the other hand, James, speaking by the Holy Spirit concerning the Gentiles, says that "God at the first did visit the Gentiles, *to take out of them a people for his name*," and "after this will I re-turn. . . . that the residue of men might seek after the Lord, and *all the Gentiles, upon whom my name is called, saith the Lord*" (Acts 15:14, 17). Here, again, is first an elective out-gathering and then a total in-gathering.

Now, by looking at other scriptures, it seems clear that the Holy Spirit is the divine agent in both these redemptions, the partial and the total. If we refer to Joel's great prophecy, *"I will pour out my Spirit upon all flesh,"* and then to Peter's reference to the same recorded in Acts, we are led to ask whether this prediction was completely ful-filled on the day of Pentecost. Clearly not. Peter, with in-spired accuracy, says, *"This is that which was spoken by the prophet Joel,"* without affirming that the prophecy of Joel had been entirely fulfilled. Turning back to the pre-diction itself, we find that it includes within its sweep "the great and the terrible day of the Lord" and the bringing "again the captivity of Judah and Jerusalem" (Joel 2:31; 3:1). These events are clearly in the future. If we examine again the vivid prophecy of Israel's conversion, we observe that their looking upon Him whom they pierced, and mourning for Him, follows the pouring out "upon the house of David, and upon the inhabitants of Jerusalem, the Spirit of grace and supplication" (Zech. 12:10). This is how Scrip-ture pictures desolations of Jerusalem, and indeed this is how it has actually existed during the present age. Ac-cording to the prophet, this judgment of thorns and briars and forsaken palaces and desertion of population will con-tinue "until the Spirit be poured upon us from on high" (Isa. 32:15).

Indeed the Scriptures seem to be harmonious in teaching that after the present elective work of the Spirit has been completed, there will come a time of universal blessing when the Spirit shall literally be "poured out upon all flesh." At that time "that which is perfect shall come" and "that which is in part shall be done away."

For this reason there is in the doctrine of the Spirit a constant reference to the final consummation. "The Holy Spirit of God, whereby ye are sealed *unto the day of redemption*," says Paul (Eph. 4:30). Again: "Ourselves also, which have the first-fruits of the Spirit, even we ourselves groan within ourselves, waiting for the adoption, to wit, *the redemption of our body*" (Rom. 8:23).

All that the Comforter has already brought us or can now bring us is only the first sheaf of the great harvest of redemption awaiting us on our Lord's return. "Ye have received *the Spirit of adoption*, whereby we cry, Abba, Father" (Rom. 8:15); but for the adoption itself we wait; sons of God already by birth from above, we with the whole creation yet wait for "*the manifestation of the sons of God*" (Rom. 8:19).

A revealing illustration is added to James's tender exhortation to be patient until the coming of the Lord: "Behold, the husbandman waiteth for the precious fruit of the earth, and hath long patience for it, until he receive the early and latter rain" (James 5:7). As in husbandry the one rain belonged to the time of sowing and the other to the time of harvest, so in redemption the early rain of the Spirit was at Pentecost and the latter rain will be at the Parousia. The one fell upon the world as the first sowers went forth into the world to sow. The other will accompany "the harvest which is the end of the age," and will prepare the earth for the final blessing of the age to come. It will bring repentance to Israel and the remission of sins, that "the times of refreshing shall come from the presence of the Lord; and he shall send Jesus Christ, which before was preached unto you: whom the heavens must receive until the times of restitution of all things" (Acts 3:19–21).